the mommy diaries

finding yourself in the daily adventure

compiled by Tally Flint

with foreword by Naomi Cramer Overton

Revell

a division of Baker Publishing Group
Grand Rapids, Michigan

© 2008 by MOPS International

Published by Revell
a division of Baker Publishing Group
P.O. Box 6287, Grand Rapids, MI 49506-6287
www.revellbooks.com

Second printing, May 2008

Printed in the United States of America

Library of Congress Cataloging-in-Publication Data

The mommy diaries : finding yourself in the daily adventure / compiled by Tally Flint ; with foreword by Naomi Cramer Overton.
    p.   cm.
    ISBN 978-0-8007-3287-5 (pbk.)
    1. Mothers—Religious life. I. Flint, Tally.
BV4529.M595 2008
248.8'431—dc22   2008006972

Contents

Foreword

Naomi Cramer Overton

It says in my diary,

> *January 8, 2001. Something's around the corner for me. I'm going to lose this baby weight, come back here, and climb Half Dome.*

"Here" was Yosemite National Park, and the rest of my family and our friends were off snowboarding. Everyone was having a great time. Except me.

I was with my two-year-old daughter, Katriel, riding the bus around and around Yosemite's valley floor. In addition to her company, I was hanging out with thirty extra pounds of padding, courtesy of having been pregnant with twins.

Brring. I yanked the cord to get off the bus to try a small adventure, a part-mile walk back to the motel. Off Katriel raced to climb a railing, and I ran to steady her. And then I looked up.

Up above our heads lilted a wispy waterfall. How had I missed it before? I secured Katriel in my arms and scanned

A Song of Ascents

I lift up my eyes to the hills—
    where does my help come from?
My help comes from the LORD,
    the Maker of heaven and earth.
He will not let your foot slip—
    he who watches over you will not slumber;
indeed, he who watches over Israel
    will neither slumber nor sleep.
The LORD watches over you—
    the LORD is your shade at your right hand;
the sun will not harm you by day,
    nor the moon by night.
The LORD will keep you from all harm—
    he will watch over your life;
the LORD will watch over your coming and going
    both now and forevermore.

Psalm 121

the valley. There stood a mountain that looked like it had been chopped in half. I eyed it and strangely heard myself saying, "I will climb that one day." One day. One day soon. I had never done something like that before, but I had heard it was fun and thrilling. I *needed* thrilling.

Feeling hopeful, I kicked leaves with Katriel on the walk back to our motel room. Once inside, I busied her with a favorite toy and grabbed my diary. I had to record this: I *would* climb Half Dome.

Cheap motel pen in hand, I recorded a dream, a goal, a prayer. I sensed God had something around the corner for me—was it having my longed-for fourth child, I wondered? Even though I was enjoying my daughter, Katriel, her twin had died during pregnancy and I still struggled with feeling sad and wondering what life would be like if she had lived. Or would I discover an exciting new job? All I knew was that it was time to begin, to leave the cocoon of overwhelmed feelings and grief. It wasn't about having a fit body or enjoying my looks while I still had some. It was some other kind of unwrapping—preparing for a new season of life while living more fully in this one.

As I left the national park a few days later, I urged my husband, "Let's stop there." At the roadside knickknack shop, I bought a small magnet with a picture of Half Dome on it. I tucked it inside my diary and later posted it on my refrigerator.

That January 8, I started moving toward my goal. Fast-forward six years, to another diary entry after that small beginning:

January 8, 2007. Six years ago today, I began preparing for the next season. Today I met with [TOPS International CEO] Elisa Morgan and felt completely at peace about moving forward to explore possibly leading TOPS.

Six years from a small beginning to a big meeting. To the day. Exactly.

Perspective and identity began in the valley, with small choices—getting off the bus to notice, looking up to gain perspective, recording hope in a diary, and marking it with a magnet on my fridge. None of it felt easy, but it helped me see who I was, what mattered, and how to walk into the future.

In the stories that follow, we ride in the valleys—and glimpse views from the heights—with other moms. Unlike the diaries I treasured as a young girl, these don't have teensy locks with easily misplaced keys. Rather they are open to us, and for us, to help us become the women, moms, and influencers our families, our communities, and the world so need us to be.

Naomi

P.S.: On June 15, 2002, I did climb Half Dome. Later I climbed the Grand Teton, and that trek sent thousands of dollars overseas to help children orphaned by AIDS. I'm still climbing, and I still have days in the valleys, and I'm doing both in good company.

I Can't Wait

When you reach the proper age
I will teach you to read and you can turn the pages
How to dress and tie your shoes
Your one plus ones, and your two times two's
And you'll teach me
Of hearts and dreams
And all the most important things
And all that I have lost along the way
And I can't wait

As you grow, I'll show you things
How to ride your bike and kick your legs out on the swings
To fold your hands and bow your head
To say your prayers before you go to bed
And you'll teach me
Of hearts and dreams
And all the most important things
And all that I have lost along the way
And I can't wait

How do you sleep so peacefully?
How do you trust unflinchingly?
How do you love so faithfully?
How do you dance so joyfully?
And you'll teach me
Of hearts and dreams
And all the most important things
And all that I have lost along the way
And I can't
No I can't
Come teach me
Of hearts and dreams
And all the most essential things
And all that I have lost along the way
And I can't wait

1   Identity

Owning My Adventure

Wife. Mother. Daughter. Sister. Friend. Moms wear a lot of different hats and fulfill a multitude of roles in any given day. As we shift from personality to personality, it can be hard to remember who we really are—at our core. Life changes us, but despite any maturation, wisdom, and perspective we might gain, our core remains the same. The personhood we were born with stays with us our whole lives through. Our deepest desires, passions, and traits seek outlet as much as ever, even if they are buried deep beneath a mothering exterior.

The practical life of a mom can certainly bring a crashing halt to some of the ways we previously lived out our core values. A woman who used to spend hours a day with her nose stuck in a good book finds it challenging to read a chapter a week between caring for her infant and her rambunctious toddler. But she does manage to join a monthly book club that feeds her love of literature in a way that doesn't clash with her family life. A dedicated runner may not be able to enjoy her old three-hour-long runs each day, but she can envision a scenario that involves her child, a jogging stroller, and an invigorating workout. Without a doubt, we have to get creative about tending to ourselves once babies come along. But by doing so, we grow into the fullness of our true identity.

Who we are serves as a map to guide our journey as adults. Veering from the map leaves us feeling lost, unfulfilled, and inept. But when we do stay on course, our life flows out of who we were created to be. Each task and accomplishment bears the unique fingerprint of our soul. We discover a role only we can fill, an adventure only we can live. That's when we truly soar and make the most influential impact we can on this world. We might very well be our husband's wife, our children's mother, and our parents' daughter. But we're first, undeniably, our *self*.

> I am a woman above everything else.
>
> —Jacqueline Kennedy Onassis

The High Chair Day

by Jane Rubietta

I peeled back the covers and leapt from bed at the sound, unusual so early in the morning. Silence. Absolute, glorious silence. Our rural home shared airspace with a grain elevator, and in keeping the grain dry twenty-four hours a day, it roared like a hair dryer aimed at earring level. Add to that the constant chatter of two children two and under, and the sum total is one frustrated woman. One frustrated woman with a grain-bin full of guilt. Because a good mother loves to be with her children. A good mother wants nothing for herself. With rules like that, a good mother ... quickly turns sour, like milk left on the counter on a hot summer day. And I'd been on the counter too long. On the counter with two children and no emotional space.

I rushed from bed in the luscious silence, the wondrous hush of pulsating eternity, and crept down the stairs. Alone! For the first time in two years, I felt like a human being rather than a mother only. The silence invited me back to my soul.

Once babies are born, priorities shift. No longer are we our first concern. And this is a good, growing, turning point. Our helpless infants become our raison d'etre, our reason for being. And while we are helping them grow emotionally, physically, and spiritually, it is so easy to neglect the same growth frontiers in our own lives. The result may not be pretty.

That morning in our little country kitchen, I breathed in the quiet. I plopped at the table with my Bible and a notebook for recording great wisdom and words revealed in the silence.

And then I saw the list. I forced myself away from the list, because this was errand day and the list was long. We had one car, and my husband used it for his fifteen-hour workdays. Every couple of weeks I scheduled use of the car, expressed breast milk, and gathered diaper bag, books, snacks, the banking, any necessary returns, the ever-present and ever-lengthening list, and the two children, and I headed off to town for hours of running.

My anxiety climbed like mercury. "Don't look at the list," I coached myself. "Don't look at the list." Back to my Bible, back to this soaking quiet.

And then I heard whistling. My standard rule for parenting is this: do not awaken a sleeping child, or I will kill you (figuratively speaking). And here was my sweet, handsome, kind husband whistling down the stairs. Stairs, a perfect conduit for the travel of sound. Stairs, whisking the whistling noise straight to the children's rooms.

I tried to be kind when he came through the kitchen door. I tried to love him. Until I saw the piece of paper in his hand. "Hon, when you go to town, would you mind picking up . . . ?"

My unstable emotional cart tipped. I jumped from my chair and screamed, "What do you think I am? Your *servant*?" This would have been a good place to stop. But no. I picked up the high chair . . . and started banging it on the kitchen floor.

Rich's eyes widened; his mouth closed. He backed from the room. He is a wise and discerning man. He has never mentioned my outburst, my breakdown, my wretched ugliness. But beneath my hammering pulse, I felt sick. I sank down at the table, where my Bible and notebook reproached me, and wept.

How had I gotten to the point of such hollowness that such a small request would push me over the edge? I'd lost myself in the parenting equation. In those rules for good mothers, no one told me that my identity as a woman needed attention, just like my kids. That morning, slammed by shame, I took inventory. If who I am is what I do, well, I spent a lot of time changing diapers, shoveling food off the floor, and feeding neighborhood children. Once I commended my child on finishing his vegetables. All of them. In about four seconds. Then I noticed his nose seemed misshapen.

He'd stuffed his vegetables into his tiny nostrils. If who we are is what we do, I was in trouble. Picking vegetables out of children's noses did not seem like a balanced or even meaningful identity base.

I knew I wanted to grow in my role as a mother. I hadn't realized that if I want to grow in my roles, I first needed to grow in my soul. That morning my inventory revealed seriously bare emotional cupboards. No one fed into my life; no wise women mentored me. My reading consisted of board books and occasionally a fast-food Scripture, but no serious depth reading that nurtured my soul or emotional needs.

I said yes to everything that came along. Yes to the person wanting to offer a party-plan home show. Yes to the leaderless committee at church. Yes to the substitute Sunday school teaching. Yes to the undones my husband couldn't finish. Yes to the neighbors, yes to anyone, everyone—because good women said yes. But I never said yes to myself.

This partially explained my hunger that morning for silence, my spurting anger over one more request for help. My rage was over my lost self. We react out of our wounds. In the stillness, I acknowledged the wounds behind the anger. I needed help working through some ancient pain, so I sought a support group. Each Thursday for a few hours was my own, and if Rich wasn't free to be with the children, then I swapped time with a neighbor. I created boundaries to protect this fragile person developing within me, just as I would protect my own children. I never said yes to anyone else on Thursday night because healing was my first emotional priority.

And with equal vigilance I guarded time each morning for my soul. If a boundary protects the unique identity God has given each one of us, then we are the only people who can do that for ourselves. Kids, husband, neighbors, church—these people will not protect that special identity.

That high chair day began an internal listening process. Parts of me were dying, withering away like muscles long ignored. Gifts I neglected, hopes I discarded, interests I set aside that brought life and rounded out my soul. To listen better, I started journaling for emotional, spiritual, and artistic health, taking notes on my soul, on my parenting mess-ups, on my disastrous attempts at wholeness. I practiced noticing sunsets and describing them, and I read everything possible out loud to the children. Journaling taught me to notice my needs, to practice honesty, to work through emotional radioactivity.

Children's voices, sweet and strident as they are, drown out those internal longings. Who else are we, besides mothers? What hopes and gifts nestle inside, buried treasure waiting for discovery? Creating space to listen helps us to develop those gifts and hopes.

As a woman who put great stock in doing for others and ignoring herself, I needed enormous practice in *becoming*— being the woman I was called to be, before a husband and children took up residence in my heart. It's a lifelong process. Thankfully, death is the only deadline.

After that morning, the high chair leaned dangerously to one side, requiring the children to brace themselves against the opposite side of the high chair. Food always slid to the right of the tray. I love the balancing act required by the high chair. How fitting that my own rebalancing began with such an out-of-balance event.

Finding Myself at Disney World
by Liz Curtis Higgs

At least once during our childhood, most of us heard our exasperated mothers say, "Someday I hope you have a daughter *just like you.*" I always wondered if such words were a veiled threat . . . or an unfinished confession on my mother's part. Maybe she was just like *her* mother. Was that a bad thing, to see ourselves in our daughters?

When I gave birth to my sweet Lillian, a new question arose: If she *was* just like me, would that make loving her easier or harder? Would we get along or always be at odds? Would life with Lillian be fun or frazzled? I discovered the answer when my daughter turned five.

For Miss Lillian's birthday, I cashed in some frequent flyer miles and arranged a trip for two to Orlando, just us girls. She talked of nothing else for weeks. I was excited too but also a bit apprehensive about traveling with my ultra-picky, slightly prickly, just-like-me daughter.

Ready or not, the big day came and off we went. To my astonishment and delight, Lillian was an angel. She flirted with the pilots, entertained the passengers, and carried on a non-stop conversation with her stuffed pony, Brownie, who always got the window seat. We spent our first afternoon in Orlando at SeaWorld, where my animal lover was beside herself with joy, watching Shamu and friends leap and splash.

The next day, however, dawned gray and rainy. "Not today, Lord," I grumbled, as Lillian and I climbed into our special new Disney World outfits. "Not the Magic Kingdom in a thunderstorm."

Yup. There were no ponchos to be found for miles around, so a little fold-up umbrella was all we had between the monsoon and us. If I was worried that all the rain would dampen my daughter's enthusiasm (and I was), I hadn't counted on her amazing ability to go with the watery flow.

We did Dumbo the Flying Elephant in an absolute downpour, laughing all the way, and sailed through It's a Small World, where every turn produced a "Wow! Look at that!" Next we fought a tempest in the Teacups, then made our way through the Haunted Mansion with Lillian's head firmly buried in my chest.

Through it all, she was a trouper. Even with sheets of rain running down her face, she looked up at me, eyes sparkling, and said, "Mom, we're having a great time, aren't we?" Where, I wondered, did all this fortitude come from?

When the sun suddenly appeared for Mickey's three o'clock parade, Lillian wiggled and charmed her way up front to take it all in. I watched her shout with glee as the band came by, and I found tears sneaking down my cheek. Oh, that pixie! So full of joy, such an unflagging spirit. Was I like that too? Or did we share only my less-than-lovely traits?

By dinnertime, when she finally ran out of gas, we made our way back to the hotel as the rains returned in earnest. That night, fresh from the tub and wrapped in her cotton pajamas, she fell asleep in my arms soon after we curled up to watch a movie. I watched the screen, but mostly I watched Lillian. Skin as smooth as silk. Long lashes fanned across her pink cheeks. Curly, dark blond hair ringed her sweet face. If you look up *cherub* in the dictionary, you might find her five-year-old face pictured there.

I'd never felt such mother love as I felt that night, pouring out like rain. Not because Lillian is beautiful (which, of course, she is), nor because she's clever and creative and charming. At that precise moment, I fell in love with my daughter for who she truly is, not for what I hoped she might be. I embraced all the ways we were different and all the ways we were the same.

> What lies behind us and what lies before us are small matters compared to what lies within us.
> —Ralph Waldo Emerson

In doing so, I embraced my own childhood self, long buried. That chubby little preschooler who refused to be discouraged. That not-always-popular girl who wore her heart on her sleeve. That rebellious teenager who swore she'd never have children.

Good girl, bad girl, real girl.

When I discovered a fresh wellspring of love for my precious Lillian, I also discovered I could love and accept her mother, flaws and all. Someday I hope Lillian has a daughter *just like her.*

Control Release
by Elisabeth Selzer

I stood trembling as I listened to my daughter rev up again to more piercing screams, her pencil-straight locks sticking to her damp forehead. She had been crying in varying degrees of pitch for two straight hours, and in my sleep-deprived state, I could not see a way to stop her crying. I had changed her, fed her, burped her, checked her temperature—and still nothing would stop the wails. I realized that no matter how I tried or what I tried, this little being, who had once been a part of me, would not stop crying. When I gave birth to her, I had left a world of easy personal control for a new world of feeling helpless at the cries of an infant. The cries continued to pierce the thick air of my exhaustion. I felt my hands gripping her arms tightly, too tightly. I looked at her and wanted to scream back, to shake some sense into her. She was stretching the fine thread of composure I had left, and it was about to snap.

Then a small voice in the back of my weary mind said, "Put her down." Briefly my head cleared. I looked in horror at the tense grip I had around Sammi's little arms. I quickly laid her in her bassinette, withdrawing my hands as if I had touched a hot stove. What was wrong with me? How had I let things get to this point? At that moment, I could have hurt this precious child my husband and I had thought I would never be able to conceive. I felt so ashamed. Stumbling out

the mommy diaries

of the room, I shut the door to muffle the cries, knowing she was safe for the moment. I wilted against the wall, resting finally on the cold tile, and wept.

I could not control this situation, could not make it right. I felt like such a bad mother, first because I could not make her stop crying and then because I had believed myself above the desperation of reaching my very limit. For most of my life, I had been about control. I controlled everything from what I wore to how I spent my time to what my apartment looked like. I controlled when I slept and when I ate, and I enjoyed carefully planned leisure time. Naively, I had thought having a baby would not add much to my daily routines—I had a four-year-old from my husband's previous marriage, and part-time motherhood had been great fun.

But what I faced now with this precious new life, this unpredictable bundle of contradictions, was bringing me to my knees. I had to realize I was not invincible; I could not control everything, particularly not this unpredictability of naps, diaper eruptions, illness, and yes, crying fits. I had to let go. I needed to exert control by relinquishing it.

This would mean letting the dust bunnies sit or pulling back my greasy hair when a shower just wasn't in the cards. I had to realize that being the mother of a baby is time-consuming and that each day showed little tangible proof of the hours of care and devotion to temporary things—that diapers and clothes just get dirty again, hours of crying bouts soothed soon begin again, and meals vanish except for the reminder left by the dirty dishes in need of washing. I needed to let go of my desire to have tangible evidence of my work and instead focus on something different: the importance of raising children who are loved and cared for and who grow up to be positive contributors in life. I can control the value I place on that over other things.

Just realizing how my need for control was clouding my enjoyment of one of the most precious times in my child's life helped my perspective significantly. I had known that raising strong, happy, confident children is worth anything I had to give up, but the day-to-day proved challenging. Letting go of my need for control was a helpful first step—a first step in changing who I've always been to becoming who God wants me to be. I'm learning to be a woman who can let go of control and enjoy the precious, sometimes uncontrollable, moments that life as a mother offers.

Whispered Essentials
by Diane Jasper

Our relaxed movie night was shattered by the panicked shriek, "Mom, I have to go potty!" My three-year-old daughter was jumping up and down, too frantic to think. I leaped from the couch, scooped her up, and raced for the bathroom. But the booster seat was upstairs. Holding horrified Audrey out at arm's length, I flew up the stairs to the other bathroom, fearing the wet burst that might drench us any second.

Meanwhile, her grandma rolled on the couch, laughing hysterically as she watched us race by, both our faces stretched tight in a matching grimace. She was no help whatsoever.

When we finally made it upstairs, with the emergency now past, Audrey was in no hurry to finish her business. She sat and played and fiddled, while I was impatient to get back to the movie. She coached me, "Mom, we just have to wait till I'm done, remember?" *Yes*, I remembered with an impatient sigh. Finally she finished, and I hurriedly ran through the rest of the routine of our Potty Essentials: wipe, flush, wash, soap. "Good job. Let's go."

"Did you make it?" Grandma asked with a smirk as I collapsed back on the couch.

"Yes. You'd think something as basic as potty training would be easier," I complained. "I'll be glad when we don't have this panic all the time."

"Don't worry, Diana; you'll both get it figured out."

That same night my cuddle bug climbed in bed with me, her sweet little face pressed close to mine on the pillow. Soon her wiggling woke me up enough that I got up to go to the bathroom. As soon as I lay back down next to her sleepy face, I heard her whispering.

"Did you wait?" Even half asleep she waited for an answer.

"Yes."

"Did you wipe?"

"Yes."

"Did you flush?"

"Yes."

"Did you wash your hands?"

"Yes."

"Did you use soap?"

"Yes."

"Good job."

I grinned silently to hear my oft-repeated reminders whispered back at me by my precious sleeping angel. My persistence must have made a deep impression in her. I was surprised she could literally say them in her sleep. *"At least she knows what to do. Now she just has to remember,"* I thought as I closed my eyes to sleep.

Suddenly I was wakened by a different whisper. God was speaking quietly and gently to my inner spirit, my heart. He was reminding me of *his* essentials, basic things I learned long ago but had somehow forgotten.

"Diana, do you know I love you?"

"Yes, Lord, I do."

"Do you know you are mine?"

"Yes!"

"Do you know I am with you?"

"Yes."

Tears came to my eyes and my heart glowed with the warmth of this loving reminder. How was it that the almighty God was taking time to speak to me in this precious, intimate way?

The tone changed and became more instructive.

"Did you talk to me today?"

"God, you know I didn't."

"Did you read my Word?"

"I was too busy."

"Even so," God's quiet whisper persisted, *"hold on to these truths:* I love you. You are mine. I am with you. *Learn to live in them. They are your Life Essentials that will keep you strong step by step, so you won't need to panic or feel alone or be afraid. Even when you have to wait."*

I lay there glowing in the dark, awestruck by this fresh burst of grace. God began showing me how I let the rush and panic of grown-up life pull me away from my Life Essentials. I belong to an amazing God who loves me. *Me, Diana!* That changes everything! I want to *live* in this, and *remember* it, so next time I will hear God whisper, *"Good job. Let's go!"*

It's Me I Like!
by Elisa Morgan

When my kids were tiny, I looked forward to a half hour of TV every weekday. No, it wasn't a soap opera. No reruns of *Friends*. Not even *Oprah* or *Dr. Phil* (they didn't exist then).

My favorite half-hour of TV was *Mister Rogers' Neighborhood*. Each day after nap time I'd place my toddlers, snack in lap, in front of the tube and switch on my friend. They thought it was their time, but it was really for me.

Mister Rogers strolled into his living room, hung up his jacket, put on his red sweater, replaced his street shoes with tennis shoes, and then sat down to tell me about life. I remember stories about sharing and about friends. I remember songs and finger plays which acted out lessons of forgiveness and hope. But most of all I remember that Mister Rogers liked *me*. Looking past the disarray of my preschool plague— Lego-littered carpet, makeup-less and sweat-panted me— he'd sing a song which has stayed with me to this day:

> *It's you I like.*
> *It's not the things you wear,*
> *It's not the way you do your hair—*
> *But it's you I like!*

Sometimes I was still in my jammies when he came on at 4:00 p.m. On some afternoons, my attitude was stinkier than my toddlers' diapers. And in some moments I actually glared at the TV from the stack of laundry which had taken over my day and time. Still, he sang out hope and acceptance.

Each time he sang this song, I pondered his words and wondered at their truth. I knew that Mister Rogers was actually a Presbyterian minister who viewed his television show as an opportunity to share God's love with his audience. Did he know I was watching? Was there *really* someone who liked *me* just for *me*?

Indeed. Mister Rogers reminded me of what I'd learned earlier in my life, as a teenager first beginning my spiritual journey toward God: God truly loves me just the way I am. He looks beyond the things I wear and the way I do my hair and likes the *me* he made. Mister Rogers reached across my preschool-days preoccupation and reminded me that God sees *beauty* in what he has made in me. Even when I feel like I'm not producing, I'm not nice, and I'm not pretty, God likes *me*. He still does.

> The most wonderful thing about Tiggers is I'm the only one!
> —A. A. Milne

Miss Crystal
by Crystal Bowman

As a young married woman with no kids, I enjoyed being a preschool teacher. It was a fun career, and it was very good for my self-esteem. Most preschoolers adore their teacher—and since the children loved me, the parents loved me too. I was showered with flowers, candy, and gifts at Christmastime, Valentine's Day, and even at the end of the school year.

the mommy diaries

The children affectionately called me Miss Crystal, and I felt loved and appreciated.

After five years of teaching preschool, I gave birth to our first child and began my new career as a stay-at-home mom. Being a mother of preschool children is much different than being a teacher of preschool children. Even though I could easily manage fifteen kids in the classroom, I found that having three kids at home was emotionally and physically overwhelming. In the classroom, I followed routines and schedules and released the kids to their parents at 3:00 p.m. At home, my days and nights were an ongoing series of unpredictable events and unscheduled visits to the pediatrician's office. At times I was pulled in so many different directions I wasn't sure which way to turn.

Even though the preschool years seemed like an eternity at the time, they didn't last forever. When my kids were finally in school, my days became somewhat more orderly and manageable—still very busy, but not quite so crazy. I knew I had it good—I was blessed with a loving husband and wonderful kids, and I knew I was loved and appreciated. But somewhere along the way I felt like I had lost my identity. In the business world I was known as Bob's wife. At my kids' school, where I often volunteered, I was known as Robby, Scott, and Teri's mom. In my heart and mind I knew that being a wife and mother was my greatest calling ever. But sometimes I wondered who I was—deep down inside.

Then one weekend my husband came home from a business seminar with a renewed zest for life. With great enthusiasm he shared how important it is to identify and develop our talents and passions. He begged me to fill out a questionnaire which would help me discover my inner desires. My first reaction was that I didn't need a survey to help me discover anything about myself. My talent was that I could feed, clothe, and love one husband and three children. My passion was that I longed for an uninterrupted nap. Who needs to know more than that?

I finally agreed to my husband's wishes and carefully answered dozens of thought-provoking questions. Even though I was a skeptic from the beginning, I have to confess that God used this experience to show me who I was—deep down inside. I discovered that my passion was writing. And even though I had been writing since I was ten years old, I had never seen myself as a "real" writer or thought of it as a God-given talent.

I had always enjoyed writing as a casual hobby, but my writing took on a deeper meaning and purpose while raising my three little ones. From the time they were born I kept journals for each of them. I didn't write in them every day, but when they would say or do something humorous or precious, I captured the moment forever on the pages of their journals. For example, when Robby was two years old, I took him with me to vote in a presidential election. After I finished voting he asked, "Did we just get married?"

And when I brought Teri home from the hospital, three-year-old Scott looked at her tummy and asked, "When is her extension cord going to come off?"

Those were the kinds of moments that made picking up my pen and paper worth the effort. Birthday parties, holidays, vacations, and everyday adventures with my children also provided rich words and images for the empty pages begging to be filled. In addition to writing in my kids' journals, I often wrote poems and prayers in my own personal journal and found it to be a therapeutic outlet for the joys and struggles of motherhood.

What I didn't realize until I spent quality time with the questionnaire was that while I was writing about the lives of my children, God was shaping me and preparing me for the "real" world of writing.

"My inner desire is writing," I announced to my husband after that profound discovery. My husband then suggested that I pursue getting published. It was a scary thought, but I felt I had to at least give it a try. While my kids were in school, I had a few hours during the day to focus on my writing and my new dream of publishing. I was ecstatic when I received an offer to write lyrics for children's piano music and even more ecstatic when I was given the opportunity to develop and write an early reader series for a Christian publishing company.

As the writing doors continued to open, I was never at a loss for ideas. Whenever I needed a burst of creativity for a new story, I opened my desk drawer and flipped through my kids' journals. As I read excerpts of winter expeditions in the backyard woods and indoor

> For we are God's workmanship, created in Christ Jesus to do good works, which God prepared in advance for us to do.
> Ephesians 2:10

picnics in the basement, writer's block was never an issue. My greatest resources were not a dictionary or thesaurus; they were the journals I had been keeping for the past ten years.

I first started writing professionally nearly two decades ago, and I am humbled and amazed by the many writing opportunities God has given me. I no longer wonder who I am because I *know* who I am. I am still Bob's wife, and I am still Robby, Scott, and Teri's mom—although I no longer need to feed and clothe them. I am a child of God, and I'm a writer of children's books. And that's just as good as being Miss Crystal.

Dance Fever
by Laryssa Toomer

I have a secret: I love music, especially disco. I love dancing to this music even more. The simple thought of the *Saturday Night Fever* movie poster and Bee Gees music puts a smile on my face and a quick dance pep in my step.

As a pastor's kid, I used to stand in front of my bedroom mirror and re-teach my dad's sermons. When I finished, I danced and pretended I was Donna Summer performing on *American Bandstand*. This strong musical influence from the 1970s and '80s frequently inspired some of the dance moves on our cheerleading squad in high school. But as much as I enjoyed dancing, I somehow suppressed this passion as I became an adult, writing it off as "something of the past." I also feared what my fellow Christian sisters might think of me, possibly seeing me as "less spiritual" if they knew my secret.

Traveling from place to place as a military wife, I often surfed radio stations on long drives. Whenever I found an oldies station, my husband and I immediately started to sing, snap our fingers, and laugh as we reminisced about music and dances of the past. It brought a special kind of happiness to my life, so why didn't I listen and dance more?

the mommy diaries

> **Surround Yourself with Things That Bring You Joy**
>
> Decorate your home with snapshots of family, friends, and places that make you feel happy. A favorite pet. A cherished seashore. A beautiful tree. Remind yourself daily of simple pleasures and take time to focus on your own joys (not ones assigned to you by other people in your life).

Being partial to worship music and contemporary Christian music, I had neglected the other music that moved me—the music that compelled me to pick up my spatula-turned-microphone and sing at the top of my lungs while dancing into a sweat. I determined to unashamedly and openly recapture my love for the music of my youth.

This newly found freedom has now become a routine in our family. At five o'clock in the afternoon as I prepare for dinner, I turn on the radio or television to an oldies station and listen to disco and oldies music with my children. I boogie to my heart's content for at least twenty minutes while teaching my children how to do "the bump," how to strike the John Travolta *Saturday Night Fever* pose, and how to make a *Soul Train* line. I even created a special folder on my iPod dedicated specifically to "oldies," which makes for interesting power walks.

My children initially found disco dancing humorous and asked, "What does *boogie* mean?" Now they get a kick out of screaming with me, "Booooo-geeeeeee!" Our new dancing ritual brings many laughs to our home, joy to my heart, and exciting quality time with my children. More importantly, I realized that it was okay to simply be me and to share the *real* mom with my children.

Identity

Baking Blues

by Elsa Kok Colopy

I was never one to bake cookies. Occasionally I baked some from the pre-prepared rolls at the grocery store, but even that didn't work well—only half the cookie dough ever made it into the oven. So I was at a loss when my daughter's teacher sent out a request for parental volunteers. They offered the typical cookie-baking and shape-cutting options, plus the opportunity to be a party helper. Nothing fit. I had a bad feeling the whole school mom thing wasn't going to work for me.

"Mom," Sam said, "you can tell a story!"

I shook my head. "No, I don't think so."

"Mom," Sam argued, "you make up the best stories! You write stories for other people. Mom, you're a storyteller person! It's perfect!"

I looked into my girl's big hazel eyes. "Sam, the stories I tell you are goofy. That's why I tell them under the cover of darkness—in your room with no one else around. They don't make any sense. Besides," I said, "I make funny noises and do weird things with my face. No one should be exposed to that."

"Mommmmm," Sam said, "I like your funny noises. They make me laugh my snort laugh."

I giggled. "I do love it when you snort."

"I'll do it all the time if you tell a story to my class, Mama."

"But I could bake cookies . . ."

Sam rolled her eyes. Even at six years old, she knew better. "Not a good idea, Mom."

"Okay," I said, giving up. "I'll ask the teacher."

I was hoping the teacher would turn me down. Mention something about a prohibition on weird noises or funny faces. I hoped she'd be a stuffed shirt, uptight—the non-giggling type.

She was wonderful. Kind. Gracious. "We'd love to have you come!" She exclaimed. "You're a writer, right? We'd love to have a custom crafted story!"

"But I make weird noises," I said weakly.

"How about next Friday?"

All week I worried. I sat at my computer and stared at the screen. I wondered if this whole thing might scar Sam for life. What if I told a story and no one laughed? What if they made fun of Sam because of her wacky, goofy-faced mother? What if this would start Sam down the long broken road to rebellion and ultimately . . . prison?

I was in just such a state of anxiety when I caught sight of one of my own books on the bookshelf. There it was, my name on the binding. I was a writer. Born a storyteller. God had opened that door; it was part of me.

So maybe I couldn't bake the best cookie, cut the perfect shape, or plan a party, but I could do what I was made to do. And revel in my own goofiness.

I wrote the story. It was something about talking cats and popcorn balls. I included Sam in the story, along with some of her friends. Friday came and I made my weird faces and my funny sounds. The kids laughed and laughed. The teacher invited me back. The next week I included all the kids in the story. They listened for their name and cheered when they were cast into the adventure. Another week I came with nothing in hand and asked them to give me characters. I wrote their characters on the board and told them a story using their ideas. It barely made sense. It had no plot. But it was goofy and silly, and the kids loved it.

Sam beamed each time I finished. One Friday she wrapped her arms around me. "I'm glad you're my mommy," she said. Tears came to my eyes. I guess God knew what he was doing when he created me as a non-cookie-baking, non-shape-cutting mama. I was a storyteller. Sam was proud. Maybe this school mom thing wouldn't be so hard after all.

> Today you are You,
> that is truer than true.
> There is no one alive
> who is Youer than You.
> —Dr. Seuss

Who Will Protect Us?
by Scoti Springfield Domeij

"Mom, John said he's gonna kill me with his dad's gun." I went weak hearing my son's latest neighborhood bully report. As a single mom raising my two boys, I'd been displaced from our safe neighborhood to HUD housing in the hood—I grieved, wondering *Who will protect us?*

My just-walk-away-from-a-fight and how-to-deal-with-a-bully speeches sounded hollow. I did not understand the rules of this testosterone-affected neighborhood. As a child, I was a tomboy, but my son's confrontational spirit mystified me. The thought of talking to John's rough-looking father terrified me. My preference was to lock my two sons in our apartment and never let them play outside ever again.

One evening at the local McDonald's, four gang members liberally cursed at my little boys. I ignored their verbal vomit. But when Kyle screamed in pain, "He hurt me!"

the mommy diaries

the lioness instinct surged adrenaline through my body. How could a six-foot male jerk a two-and-a-half-foot toddler's ear? Swearing was one thing . . . hurting my baby was unacceptable!

If I confronted the situation, I wondered, would I end up with a knife in my gut? I felt intimidated but sensed it was important to show my boys that I would protect them. I picked up Kyle and confronted the gang members. "Who hurt you, Kyle?"

Innocent, teary-eyed Kyle pointed, "That one." I placed my hand on the almost-man, not-quite-boy's shoulder. "You hurt my son. I want you to say you are sorry." The four gang members roared with contemptuous laughter. I gently rubbed their homeboy's shoulder, looked in his eye, and firmly but kindly said, "You hurt my son. I want you to say you are sorry." I did not flinch.

As I waited for his apology, his companions continued mocking and laughing. Then Kyle's attacker spoke: "I'm sorry."

In the midst of my shock, I immediately thought, *Those words do not sound foreign to his lips. I bet he has a wonderful, God-fearing single mother at home whose heart is broken by an out-of-control son.*

Out of nowhere a police officer appeared and asked, "Did anyone see what happened?" After questioning witnesses, he asked, "Do you want to press charges?"

"It's okay. He said he's sorry," I replied. The bully looked astounded. His buddies were finally dumbfounded into silence.

As the intimidators quickly exited, I herded the boys toward the policeman's table, where we sat to

> The strength of a nation derives from the integrity of the home.
> —Confucius

eat. Uncontrollable quivering seized my insides. I asked the officer to escort us to our car. He said, "You're lucky to be alive."

Later, after we had moved to a safer neighborhood, a tough-talking military dad marched up to me, pointed to my son, and demanded, "Who is this boy's dad?"

"I am!" I announced proudly. Surprised by my strength to face such an intimidating man, I added, "What do you want?" His whining junior high son hid behind him. Everyone—except apparently his dad—knew Bully Boy was the neighborhood tormentor.

Mr. Army Dad gruffly said, "Your son . . ."

Before he could finish, I interrupted, "Excuse me, sir, but your son has been riding around the neighborhood dispensing foul, disgusting language on the little kids via that little voice box on his bike."

Mr. Army Man swung around toward his son. They marched home. With an air of triumph, my son loudly said, "Way to go, Mom!"

I cannot and do not try to replace my sons' father. However, God is my constant companion, and he protects us when risky situations confront my family. He saw our precarious circumstance at McDonald's. Thankfully, he provided backup in the form of big-time muscle—a cop and perhaps a few dozen frazzled guardian angels wondering, "What will she try next?"

> Character, not circumstance, makes the person.
> —Booker T. Washington

> Whether you think you can or think you can't, you're right.
> —Henry Ford

the mommy diaries

The New Me

by Colleen Kappeler

I've been a swimmer since I was six years old. It was who I was—not a volleyball player, not a softball player, most definitely not a runner. Swimming was part of what defined me. I was good at it; I won races and went to state championships. Certain things like that—things we grow up believing about ourselves—become part of our definition of who we are, just as other things fall in our "not me" category. Motherhood changes that definition of self; it causes us to stretch beyond our self-imposed boundaries and to take on new roles, roles that may not even fit with "who we are."

I was not a child who dreamt of motherhood. I dreamt of adventures, solo trips around the world, photography in Africa, humanitarian aid work in Asia, camping in the outback. I looked up airline tickets to Australia and tried my hand at an Outward Bound program. I wanted to act, write, be creative, and live my life my way. And then I married my husband at twenty-three and was pregnant within a year. Suddenly I was at home, making meals, changing diapers, teaching the ABCs, and planning the budget. It was so different than all I had imagined and identified with, yet I couldn't imagine not doing it. A part of me still wanted more than anything to "hit that open road," but the idea of leaving my son for even one week saddened me. As a mother, I gained a whole new definition of myself. My accomplishments became patience and well-balanced meals. My adventures were day trips with a toddler.

Truth be told, it took years of motherhood for me to find peace in my new role and with my new definition of self. For the longest time I kept looking over one shoulder, wondering what was out there and what adventure I was missing. Wondering who this new person I had become was and how to identify with her. But slowly, over time, I have found new ways to define myself. I have stretched beyond the boundaries of my old self and created a new idea of self that connected to my original one. I am creative in groups that I run for writers in a schedule that fits around my family life so that I can be a mom first and foremost. I am adventurous in the family camping trips we have begun taking and the picnics I venture out on solo with my children. I traveled the world when I flew to China to adopt our daughter.

> The value of identity of course is that so often with it comes purpose.
> —Richard R. Grant

I participate in humanitarian aid by writing and speaking on adoption. Somehow, on a path that little resembles the one I imagined for myself, through motherhood I have found my center and have finally met the dreams I held for myself.

Motherhood requires flexibility. You discover new things about yourself and rediscover old things that you thought you had to give up. My children are both under six, and the adventures are just beginning. I love the challenges they put before me. I get to experience life all over again as I go through life with them. Sometimes it feels like a second chance at being me.

Finding You . . . Every Day

We celebrate our children's uniqueness with abandon, relishing each new feat of genius, every step of creative independence. We encourage them to chase their dreams, seek out ways to practice their talents and strengths, and enjoy their passions. Why is it so hard to do the same for ourselves?

A map remains useless if left in the glove compartment. As women wired especially to live our own lives, one-of-a-kind creations tailor-made for significant impact, we owe it to ourselves and our families to fiercely protect our core identities. Our legacies flow from them, and they are what touch and move our children most intimately. Cultivate who you are; seek out ways to grow and to stimulate your true self. No one else can fill your role; no one else is prepared so perfectly to love *your* family, mother *your* children, live *your* life. You've got what it takes. It's time to get going.

> Integrity simply means not violating one's own identity.
> —Erich Fromm

Owning Your Adventure

1. What surprised you the most about yourself once you became a mother?
2. Did you find people looked at you differently than before you were a mother?
3. How do you feel you have changed since motherhood? How do you feel you are the same?
4. Are there parts of yourself you feel you've lost and you deeply desire to regain?

5. How do you define your identity? By your kids? Spouse? Career?
6. Can you believe that you were created with amazing potential and with gifts that only you can bring to the table? If not, what's holding you back from embracing this truth?

2   Growth

Stretching and Training

Backpack? *Check.* Sleeping bag? *Check.* Water purifier? *Check.* Hiking boots? *Check.* Moleskin? *Check.*

Just like any hiker setting off for a trip into the backcountry, women enter motherhood as prepared as they can be. We devour books on pregnancy, birthing, and parenting. We seek out veterans to get the lowdown on what types of bottle nipples work best, whether to buy the disposable or wool nursing pads, and just how many hooded towels we're going to need. We take prenatal classes on child birthing, breastfeeding, caring for your newborn, and even how to introduce a new baby to the family pet.

And despite all this preparation, when that little child comes into our lives, we inevitably feel ill-equipped, confused, and sometimes downright shell-shocked. Even the seasoned backpacker trusts she's going to run into surprises along the way. No matter how much training she undergoes, lugging that forty-pound pack up a steep incline still knocks the breath out of her. A sudden change in weather can wreak havoc on the best-laid plans. Instead of the training preparing us for the journey, the journey ends up training us.

We can all point to the times in our mothering journeys when we learned some new skill, coping mechanism, or truth. And we're better for it—better moms, better spouses, better friends, better *women*. Sometimes the lessons come easy, marked by warm memories of connecting with our kids. More often than not they're painful. We uncover our own nasty habits. We make mistakes. We hurt others. But while the learning proves hard, the outcome remains positive. We draw closer to those we love. We make behavior changes for the better. We come one step closer to being the woman God created us to be. Sure, we're in the business of growing successful children. But oftentimes we find we're the ones undergoing the greatest growth of all. What will we learn today?

Learning to Nurture
by Ginny Mooney Withrow

Have you ever noticed how some women are natural nurturers? When I was single, I spent a lot of time at my friend Liz's house. I would walk in and be greeted by soothing music playing all around me. I would settle down on her comfy couch and browse through the latest edition of *Real Simple* while she prepared the tea. Oh, and what kind of tea would I like to go along with the warm scones coming right out of the oven?

In contrast, when Liz would come to the townhouse that I shared with two friends, she would notice the only things in my section of the fridge were a lone grapefruit and half a Subway sandwich.

So I wasn't surprised that one day when we were discussing our futures, Liz said to me, "Ginny, I could see you marrying a single dad who already had older children. I just can't imagine you with an infant." Personally, I couldn't agree more. Liz wasn't being unkind, just stating what seemed like the obvious.

And then it happened. Love, romance, dating, marriage . . . and six months later, the baby carriage. Well, not quite. Six months later the little blue plus sign that meant the baby carriage would soon be needed. I freaked out. I made my husband run out to the store and get a second pregnancy test since I was sure it *must* be mistaken. That infant neither Liz nor I could see me with couldn't possibly be on the way . . . or could it?

One year later, I sat in Liz's cozy kitchen once again, sipping decaffeinated Earl Grey and munching on a scone. This time I was holding a wobbly, three-month-old baby girl on my lap. Liz looked at me. "I can't believe it, Gin," she said, "but that child has made a mother out of you!"

I smiled. It seemed funny since the entire first week that our daughter was at home, I kept turning to my husband and saying, "I wonder when this child's mother is coming to get her!" But really, Liz was right. Here I was wrapping, changing, snuggling, nuzzling, and breastfeeding a little infant. And seemingly doing okay. God had made me into a mother.

I'm still not a natural nurturer, but I've learned a lot. I've learned that I have it within me, even if sometimes I need to remind myself of how important it is to nurture a little one, especially in the mile-a-minute world in which we live. My motto: slow down and sit down. When I do that, it's just a few seconds before my daughter Zaley runs over and climbs up to snuggle, talk, or just be near me.

In four years of motherhood, I've learned a lot. I've learned how to have tea parties with dolls and make-believe scones, how to mold Play-Doh into every animal that was on the ark, how to read the same book for twelve nights running with convincing enthusiasm, and how to watch a movie with a child covering me instead of a blanket.

I still need my space, of course, and I still need my time alone. But when I am with my children (now two of them), I know how much they need to be nurtured and that, yes, I can do it.

Most surprising of all, I've learned to sing. I am not much of a singer, really. In fact, an old boyfriend used to say that my child's first words would be, "Mommy, please stop singing!" But when Zaley was born, I tried to remember the songs my mother had sung to me. Little by little, they began to come back. I even called my mom a few times to ask her the words or tunes I'd forgotten— "Brahms' Lullaby," "Jesus Loves Me," "Edelweiss," "Scarlet Ribbons," "Mommy's Little Girl," and "Greensleeves."

> Therefore, if anyone is in Christ, he is a new creation; the old has gone, the new has come!
> 2 Corinthians 5:17

Now almost every night when I put my four-year-old to sleep, she asks me to sing her a song and adds, "Will you rub my head too, Mommy?" So I sit on the edge of her bed, stroke her hair, think of Liz, and begin to sing, to the tune of "Brahms' Lullaby,"

Lullaby and good night
May my sweet girl sleep tight,
Lullaby, lullaby, lullaby and good night.
Lullaby, and good night
May my Zaley sleep tight,
Lullaby, lullaby, lullaby and good night.

Baby Steps

by Jennifer Prince

My feet were firmly planted on the front porch, and they felt too heavy for me to lift in order to walk. I stood in the doorway and watched as Julia held my baby. *My* baby, who was just three weeks old and looked so small and frail as she curled up in a fetal-like position, gently sleeping on Julia's shoulder.

I had taught high school science for several years, and it remained a passion of mine. The students, the experiments, and telling about the world around us all invigorated me. But nothing prepared me for what I would feel as a mother. My precious baby, Aubrey, was born in March, and I had agreed to finish out the school year after my maternity leave. So there I stood, leaving my newborn in the care of someone else.

I wrestled with leaving my daughter—not because I did not have faith in her caregiver but because the very thought of being without her for several hours felt like leaving my heart beating somewhere outside of my body. I eventually mustered up enough courage and faith to walk off the front porch as I took those steps to leave.

Even though this was eight years ago, I remember it like it was yesterday, and I have felt those feelings again time after time—the first time she cried from separation anxiety and the day I took her to her first day of school.

Just like I took a small step by leaving my daughter in the care of another, I am realizing that motherhood is a series of baby steps that need to be taken in order to prepare our children for adulthood. I am thankful for the steps that we have already taken, and I look forward to the path that the future holds—one step at a time!

> It doesn't work to leap a twenty-foot chasm in two ten-foot jumps.
>
> —American proverb

Finding Courage
by Barbara Vogelgesang

Here's one of my deep dark secrets: I am afraid of everything. Growing up, people considered me downright wimpy. I wouldn't go upstairs alone after 6:00 p.m. because I was afraid of the dark. I cringed when I saw a group of kids standing on the corner because I was frightened of them. Bullies can smell fear, so I had my share of broken glasses and stolen lunch money. I was terrified of dogs. My best friend had a German shepherd, and in the twenty-three years we lived on the same block, I only entered her house twice because of that dog.

After we were married, my husband Jim and I bought an old stone farmhouse in the middle of nowhere. We were surrounded by a dairy farm. Each night I would go around the house locking windows and doors. Jim would chuckle and ask me if I was worried about the cows breaking in. Our only bathroom was on the first floor, and when I was expecting, I would wake Jim up to come down to the bathroom with me at night. If Jim had to be away on a business trip, I would barricade the doors at night. I simply was the most fearful person I knew—until I became a mom.

Shortly after my oldest son, Nick, was born, Jim had to go on an extended trip for work. He had to leave our three-week-old and me alone in our big old house in the middle of nowhere with the only bathroom downstairs.

The first night Jim was gone, I tucked our newborn into his cradle, and something incredible happened. I found my courage. When the baby cried, I flew into the darkness, without reservation, to care for his needs. When the neighbor's dog came into our yard, I chased it away with a mama bear's intensity. I even killed a spider myself.

> The value of marriage is not that adults produce children, but that children produce adults.
>
> —Peter De Vries

When Jim got home, he noticed something was different. I wasn't the frightened little wife he had left behind. I had become a mother. I liked this new me. I was free to become so much more than the fearful woman I had been.

Nick is now fifteen, and we have three more children who still push me to overcome fears. Scaling the Mount Everest of laundry takes bravery some days. It takes that special brand of mother-courage to drop off my youngest on the first day of kindergarten. I think I'm pretty daring when I take all four kids camping. Letting my thirteen-year-old daughter go on a missions trip to an inner city without me along takes bravado.

I will be really courageous as I teach my teenage son to drive. But the most daring thing I will ever do is let my dear children grow up and pass on to them the courage they gave me.

Little Wanderer
by Angie Grella

If you happened to be looking out your window that day, I'm sure you would've been rolling on the floor, laughing, as you saw a young mother frantically running down the cul-de-sac, chasing after her little boy. I, on the other hand, was *not* laughing. I was the young mother, and this wasn't the first time my two-and-a-half-year-old son, Nathan, had made a game out of running away from me. That day, we had been playing in the front yard. We lived in a cute neighborhood, with fairly new housing, on the corner of a cul-de-sac. Lots of youngsters lived in the neighborhood, but no one seemed to be out that day when Nathan decided to be adventurous.

Nathan took off running across the street and a few houses down. (Did I mention I was about five months pregnant with our second child? That tended to slow me down a bit.) One of the neighbors had happened to leave his garage door open with a car parked inside. Little boys must have some kind of magnet that draws them to cars. Nathan ran right up the driveway into the garage. By the time I caught up with him, he had already opened the car door. Thankfully, no car alarm went off and as far as I know, no one witnessed the incident. It must have looked pretty odd, though, to see me walking my little wanderer out of someone else's garage.

My first response as a mom was relief—relief that I got there in time, relief that Nathan wasn't hurt, and relief that I didn't have to explain to my neighbor, whom I didn't know, what we were doing in his garage. But I was challenged as well on a deeper level.

Even now, a few years later, I still learn lessons from that story. As a stay-at-home mom, sometimes I *feel* like running away (Hawaii maybe?), and sometimes I *need* to get away. As an introvert, being alone energizes me. That makes summers hard. My six-year-old talks nonstop from the time he gets up. This can drain me if I don't take some time for myself, either before he gets up or while he's doing a project or having "quiet time," or just go for a walk or bike ride and leave my husband with the boys. By being aware of my needs, I'm able to find balance in giving my kids attention and giving attention to other things, like an hour of exercise. In addition, I can think of ways to involve them in what I'm doing so we can walk together through the adventure of life. Thankfully, Nathan doesn't play the "run away" game with me anymore. But just in case, keep your car doors locked!

> I like the person I am becoming.
> —Maya Angelou

Good-Bye Toddler Mom
by Cathy Penshorn

"Hey Mom, let's go," "You're going to love it," "Come on," my three-boy chorus sang as they pulled and tugged me toward the towering waterslide. This was a new phase of mothering—the follow-them-as-leaders stage instead of the follow-me-as-Mom stage. They grinned mischievously with anticipation as I studied the shimmering blue tube with white water pounding down its nearly vertical slope.

I have always been a hands-on mom: getting down on hands and knees with our boys when they crawled, digging my toes into the sandbox with them when they were pre-schoolers, and playing goalie in the face of countless practice kicks with them as they got older. I stretched them to try new experiences that moved them out of their comfort zones in those days, but now the tables had turned, and they were stretching me.

I really didn't want to do this. But I realized that I was going to have to "grow up" as a mom and leave the little-boy mom behind if I was going to be deeply connected to my "big boys." At the time, we were on the brink of full blown boyhood, a stage where the coolest thing imaginable is taking a risk or "blowing something up." Have you ever seen what happens when you embed fifty firecrackers in a watermelon? I have. How about Mentos mints in Diet Coke? Another favorite.

As my boys grew up, I had to push myself to grow with them. This meant being open to new places, new experiences, and yes, some new ideas. It meant working hard on not overreacting to most everything. It meant trying very hard to evaluate a request from their point of view and deciding to say yes whenever possible instead of saying no just because it didn't sound like fun to me.

Growing up as a mother of boys meant that I had to loosen my boundaries a bit on things that sounded (and sometimes were) "dangerous" in order to allow my boys to learn how to calculate risk. I learned to *ask* "What happens if . . .?" instead of *telling* them what would happen if. It was trial and error, and it remains so now as they navigate high school, because the world is a place full of risk and danger from which I can't protect them. So I must measure out, in best-guess doses, new opportunities for them to evaluate that danger themselves and learn from the results.

More than anything else, growing up as a mom in these ways opened my heart to facing fears deep within me—those more significant than the fear of going really fast down a waterslide. It allowed me to face the fear that when my boys had grown and my mothering was all over, I wouldn't have made a difference after all. That was the biggie, right there. I think fear of failure is one that we moms all face in some form. I decided that day at the water park to not let fear keep me from living life to its fullest. I was going to let my boys stretch me and to take some more risks. That simple decision opened a door for me to a new freedom in other areas of struggle.

So I went down the slide, screaming, several times! And you know what happened? I learned that tall waterslides are fun, that stretching isn't so bad, and that living a little more on the wild side with the guys can rejuvenate me in ways that demurely sitting by the pool with a book just can't do. I also learned that when I can honestly ask myself, "What am I really afraid of here?" on any given day about any given stressor, I am able to make better decisions and have fewer regrets.

I'm still growing, and my boys are still tugging me into new adventures with them. White-water rafting? Bring it on. Mountain biking down a ski slope? Let's go. Skydiving? I'll pass on that one and meet you at the water park. I'm not quite *that* grown up yet.

Power Struggle

by Karen Marchant

At the young age of three years old, my youngest son, John, learned that he could win a power struggle with me. The thing is, I didn't even realize we were *in* a power struggle when he slung his plate of boxed mac and cheese and canned green beans across the kitchen. I was stunned. What kid doesn't love boxed mac and cheese?

John didn't want to eat lunch, but I knew that he would soon ask for a snack. So I responded with what I believed to be a brilliant parenting move. I enlisted his help in cleaning up the mess and then said, "Until you eat some mac and cheese and green beans, you won't be able to have anything else to eat. We don't waste food in this family!"

Twenty-four hours later he hadn't eaten anything *at all*. He was staggering around the family room feeling nauseous and lightheaded. I caved and gave him a peanut butter and

the mommy diaries

honey sandwich. The joy of victory swept across his face, and at *that* moment I realized we'd been in a power struggle. The scoreboard reported *John: 1, Mom: 0.*

I realized that I needed to set realistic boundaries and consequences that could be executed successfully, allowing the children to learn and me to retain my authority. I was never going to win a battle over the clean plate club, but I could continue to provide healthy, good-tasting meal options and hold firm on a no-snack rule. I couldn't force John to eat something he didn't want to eat, but I could ensure he didn't eat junky filler foods instead. This standoff taught me that if I wanted to have a respectful and cooperative teenager, I needed to introduce consequences in the early years—but again, ones that were related to the inappropriate behavior and ones on which I could follow through.

John is now twenty years old and launching into adulthood. We don't engage in power struggles anymore. Now we're trying to maneuver our way through a relationship that is more based on friendship—my knowing when to let go and not get involved, and his knowing when to ask for help or try it on his own. Some days are better than others, and I am happy to report that John really likes boxed mac and cheese—it's one of the staples in his diet.

DEPRTONLS

by Jane Rubietta

I packed eagerly, thrilled to throw my book bag and suitcase into the car and head off to the women's leadership conference sponsored by a popular church I knew from my seminary days. My Big Girl Clothes That Grownups Wear lay neatly in the garment bag stretched out on the floor to guard against wrinkles. I brushed my teeth and lathered on makeup while our toddlers rustled about the living room, just a few steps away.

"Going on a trip." I heard a small piping voice. I peeked around the corner and saw a soon-to-be-dead child jumping on, rolling on, walking on, and otherwise wrinkling the garment bag.

I could not get out of there fast enough for their safety and my own well-being. I ground my teeth, hugged them, tugged the luggage, and cast one more glance around the room. Books, magnetic puzzles, and child-sized musical instruments littered the room, but my husband urged me onward. "Go, go. We'll be fine."

A children's musical cassette played in the background. The kids looked so happy. I blinked back tears. *What am I doing? I am a mother. I don't have any business going to this conference. I am not a leader.*

All the way to the conference, I searched for some deep wisdom. I was, after all, in the car alone, surrounded by peace and quiet. What better time to tune in to my inner self? But instead of wisdom and peace, one word filled my brain: DEPRTONLS. In caps. Not even a word, really; just a jumbled mix of letters. Desperate for learning, I wondered, what is this? Is this a word from God? Is this a secret message and I'll be given the answer later? Despite my queries, no answer came, and when I returned home from my conference, the word jumble seemed to have moved in to stay.

I readied myself to receive some truth back in my old routine. And then one day, passing by the refrigerator, I noticed the magnetic letters splattered on its door. The bottom row spelled DEPRTONLS. Great. Just what I needed—more of my family's chaotic life invading my personal space. So much for deep learning. I needed something in my mind besides a leftover row of alphabet letters.

The conference leaders had challenged me to lead wherever I found myself. And I found myself at home for very long days with two, then three, children. So I started where I could, in little ways.

I got out my seminary notes after the children went to bed, but I fell asleep at page one. I started reading some commentaries from our Smart-People's Library. My head bobbed after four sentences. Maybe I needed to start even smaller. I read the ingredient labels for food. I read board books and picture books (there's a mind-bender) and eventually graduated to paper pages with more than two words per page. But I still didn't feel any great truth seeping in.

I'd exhausted our stash of books at home, so I got us all library cards and packed in the stroller and the baby papoose every week to go to the library. We checked out truckloads of books, the maximum limit each week, and read, and read, and read. The kids learned to read by kindergarten, and I . . . I became fat with words, filled with the delight of words that don't rhyme, words with multiple syllables, words, words, words.

Reading saved my life. It saved my kids' lives. And it opened up worlds of adventure, of possibility, of hope for all of us. Reading became the centering point for our family. I read aloud with a child at my breast and two snuggled up on either side of me. I read aloud to our three children while my husband rubbed their backs and cuddled them.

And as I read, licking my lips over a rich metaphor, guzzling essays and articles and fiction and classics, the words ignited hope inside, hope that someday I too would write words. I dared to dream that those words would become a source of life to others, the life preserver thrown to the drowning mom, the sinking woman.

DEPRTONLS might not have spelled any great wisdom, but it did turn out to be a good word puzzle. By solving its mystery, I was able to inspire not only my own mind but also those of my family members. Hmm. Maybe I really have become a leader.

Sunday Grace
by Alex Kuykendall

My children determine where I sit in church. On one particular Sunday, I was in my usual spot, the last pew, convenient for extracting screaming two-year-olds. Surrounded by all the regular mommies ready to remove their own screamers at a moment's notice, I observed a young woman across the aisle. She was new to my small church's section of squirmers and shushers, but she sat apart without one of her own.

The previous Sunday our pastor had shared a story about a young married man living in our community. He had taken his own life that week, and our pastor was to perform the funeral. We had prayed for the young widow and her pain. Today, one week later, when my pastor prayed again, the visitor's sob rang out. At that moment I knew our prayers were for her, and my heart ached.

I'm not a free hugger. I don't normally touch people I don't know. And yet I felt myself moving, stepping across the aisle, handing her some Kleenex, and putting my arms around her. I didn't know if it was the right thing to do or if it would make her more uncomfortable, but my instinct forced my doubts aside. I could feel her relax a little, letting my shoulder muffle her sobs, and she didn't let go. I held on. I may not be a hugger, but I *am* a crier. My tears started with her first sob, and we cried together. I had no words, only a mother's heart: the tenderness to feel someone else's pain, to wipe tears, and to hug. Those were things I practiced daily and could offer, even to a stranger.

> I am always doing that which I cannot do, in order that I may learn how to do it.
>
> —Pablo Picasso

My children determine where I sit in church, and they positioned me in more than one way that morning. They gave me the tools needed to open my heart, step beyond my comfort zone, and freely share a hug and tears. Something I never would have done if not for them.

A Defining Moment

by Beth K. Vogt

It was not a shining moment in my life—but it was a defining one.

I recall certain details. I know my son Josh was two years old. He wore a green pair of OshKosh overalls and a gray, long-sleeved top with a white collar. At two, he was tow-headed and his eyes were more blue than hazel.

While I remember some of the visual details, the memory's sound is turned off, at least for part of the time.

I don't remember—can't hear—what I yelled at Josh that day. I don't remember why I yelled at him. I do know that I screamed loud and long. Much too loud, and much too long.

I see Josh's blue eyes widen with hurt and fear. I see him cover his face with his little hands so he can't see me. And then he turns away from me and huddles against the wall.

And *now* I can hear my son's sobs.

As I stare at his back, I come face-to-face with the stark truth: I am an angry mommy.

It's not like I'd never lost my temper before that morning. I'd yelled at my husband. My siblings. But it's one thing to dump an adult-sized load of anger onto another adult. Usually another grownup can handle a harsh word or two. He can choose to fight back, or he can leave you alone until you cool off. But a child is not equipped to deal with an adult's anger. My outburst overwhelmed my son.

Within seconds, I cradled Josh in my arms and cried with him.

"Mommy's sorry. Mommy's sorry." I whispered those words over and over again until we both stopped crying.

Faced with the reality of my anger, I had to answer two questions: *Why was I so angry? What was I going to do about it?*

Long before I was a mom, life happened. A lot of that was good. But life being what it is, I took the good and the bad—and the bad left its mark on me. Sometimes when we hurt and don't face that hurt and allow it to heal, we feel its effects years later. Once I became a mom, unhealed hurts influenced my relationship with my child. I didn't want Josh—and the other children I would later have—to grow up with an out-of-control mommy who screamed and yelled at them. And I didn't want them to act out what they experienced at home.

I wish I could say that after that wretched morning of anger and tears, I never lost my temper again. I wish I could say that with a lot of prayer and effort, I never again lost control and screamed at my children. God is a God of miracles, isn't he?

But that wasn't how God worked in my life. I sought counseling for some of the stuff that had wounded my heart. Even so, at times harsh words still spilled over onto my children. I shed many, many tears and prayed just as many prayers that God would "set a guard over my mouth" (Ps. 141:3). I asked for forgiveness each time I yelled at my precious children—again and again and again. I wasn't changed overnight—but I *was* changing. I did my part and trusted God to do his.

By the time Josh was nine years old, I no longer felt like anger controlled me. Sure, I lost my temper with Josh and his two sisters—but I felt like I fell into the "normal mom" range. We all lose our cool sometimes. And yet I still felt guilty about how I'd treated Josh when he was a preschooler. So I confessed my struggle to a close friend.

"If you're still worried about it, tell him you're sorry," she advised me. "Just be honest with him about it and ask his forgiveness."

That night, I sat on Josh's bed and struggled to find the right words. "Josh, when you were a little boy, I had a problem with anger. Sometimes I was too harsh with you. Sometimes I yelled too loud at you." My eyes filled up with tears, but I refused to look away from my son's now-hazel eyes. "I'm sorry. Will you please forgive me for being an angry mommy?" He forgave me—with a hug and a whispered, "I love you, Mom."

Eventually, I had similar talks with my two daughters— asking for their forgiveness, which they also lovingly gave me.

When Josh and his sisters were teenagers I found myself surprised—astounded!—to discover I was pregnant at age forty-one. Late-in-life motherhood was not something I ever expected to experience—but it is one of my greatest joys.

> Children seldom misquote. In fact, they usually repeat word for word what you shouldn't have said.
> —Unknown

As I try to keep pace with my "caboose kiddo," the painful memories of my early years as a mom are almost forgotten. I no longer fear the weight of my unkind words crushing my daughter's tender spirit. God has changed my heart; he has gentled my spirit. For that reason alone I am thankful God gave me the blessing of a child in my forties—to see how much he has changed me through my children. I am who I am today because I am a mom—and I am no longer an angry one.

the mommy diaries

Mississippi Epiphany
by Letitia Suk

The mighty Mississippi was quiet that sultry July afternoon. My ten-year-old daughter Christa and I were visiting
family in my hometown and had joined my sister-in-law
Karen and my niece Caroline for a spin on the river in their
outboard boat. We stretched our legs, trying to get more
comfortable, as our orange life jackets squished up around
our necks, adding to the heat of the day. Memories of growing up near this river flittered in and out of my thoughts,
but it had been a long time since I was out in the middle of
it. With no other boats in sight, Karen cut the motor and
let the craft bob in the warm water.

Suddenly Karen reached for a rope ladder and threw it over
the side of the boat, saying, "There's no river traffic today.
Let's jump in and cool off!" In a flash she was in the water,
paddling around the boat in her jacket and climbing back
up the ladder. Caroline went next, squealing with delight as
she bounced in the water before climbing aboard. Christa,
my very urban river novice, was quick to be the next one in.
From the water she called out, "Mom, come on in!"

No way was I going in, even with a life jacket. I just don't
do "jumping in the river." Didn't they know that? "Sorry, girls,
I'll just watch." Another round of jumping ensued, and soon
it was my turn again. "Pleeeease, Mom, just try!"

"No. Honey, I used to do that when I was your age"—
implying how grown up I must be—"but I don't want to
do that anymore." A shot of frustration flashed across my
daughter's face, and then she kind of shrugged and looked
away. I knew she wasn't going to ask me again.

Satisfied, I leaned back on my cushion to bask in the sun while congratulating myself that my comfort zones were still quite intact. And then it hit me: I had a choice as to how I wanted to play out decisions like this for the rest of my life. It would be safer to keep saying no, but was that really the direction I wanted to head?

Saying no to the river would soon effortlessly lead to "not today . . . no way . . . can't do that . . . won't do that" for all kinds of fabulous offers. Clutching my "no" now likely would lead to later choices to stop bike riding with my kids and to find excuses for avoiding fun outings with my friends that might stretch me a bit. Later on, a lifetime of "no" would surely lead to not wanting to drive in new places, or at all.

> Being a mother, as far as I can tell, is a constantly evolving process of adapting to the needs of your child while also changing and growing as a person in your own right.
>
> —Deborah Insel

Is that the kind of mom I want to be?

"Wait. . . . I'm coming in!" I yelled as Karen was about to pull the ladder in. Christa's face lit up with surprise and excitement, and she jumped back in again too. We all took a few more turns, laughed a lot, and soon were back on dry land talking about what we would have for dinner. A simple afternoon, but a life-changing one for me.

I soon had a chance to try out my "yes" once again when the following winter, a group of friends wanted to try snowmobiling during free time at a church retreat. My former self would have refused on the spot, but this time I gave it a whirl. Scary but fun! Saying yes to something new seems to open the next door. Saying no usually shuts it.

the mommy diaries

Who knows? Someday my grandchildren might want to go white-water rafting. In fact, I might even suggest it!

Silent Night
by Elizabeth Griffin

The slightest hint of a whimper from my dreaming four-year-old wakens me. I glanced at the clock and saw it was 2:00 a.m. The warmth of Christmas lights strung in our living room beckoned. Creeping out of bed and down our short hallway, I knelt at our couch. "I am here, Lord." Smiling, I breathed deeply and enjoyed the first few moments of soaking in his presence.

Within minutes I heard the sleeper-padded shuffle of my youngest son. He paused at the corner of the room, and I knew that because he never walks in a straight line, I had about twenty seconds to prepare myself. "Have your way in this time, Lord," I sighed, trying to surrender it with grace. The next moment my son was leaning tentatively into my back.

I turned and scooped Zachary into my lap, embracing his desire to be close. As I squeezed and massaged his feet, he pressed in and laid his head against my chest, relaxed. We sat in silence and enjoyed the way the Christmas lights transform and soften our living room.

After about ten minutes my oldest son, Taylor, shuffled into the room. I wondered how they both know instinctively where I am at all times and come without a single call—except of course, when I want them to. Yet here he was, lining up for his turn in my lap. I put Zachary back in bed, and Taylor climbed onto me. He lay across my lap like a newborn, although most of his six-year-old body now extended far beyond me. I stroked his hair and kissed his face as he drifted in and out of sleep. Looking at him, I reflected, "Lord, this is what I want with you: to come without being called and to relax in your love for me."

Once both boys were back asleep in their beds, I was tempted to return to my own. Then I heard that still small voice and returned to the couch. Now it was my turn.

My thoughts drifted back to a night so different from this peaceful interlude. It was a time when I put a lot of energy into avoiding quietness as I came to grips with our son Zachary's newly diagnosed disability. Often, in the midst of this long and painful process, I turned to other people and things to help me avoid God because I was so angry with him and it hurt too much to be quiet.

One night, after waking up overwhelmed with grief, I got out of bed and went to the computer in our office to email my sister. The email system was frozen. I rebooted the computer and tried again, but the line wouldn't go through. The whole computer froze, and I couldn't do anything at all. I became so angry that I finally got honest and began to tell God how I felt for the first time in weeks. As I ranted and raved, the tears came and I poured out my bitter heart to the Lord.

What began as a search for escape that night ended up being a time of comfort in the Lord's presence. The quietness I had been avoiding held the healing I needed. Once I poured out my heart, God quieted my tumultuous heart with his love, giving me the rest that I needed.

the mommy diaries

Find Hidden Moments of Quiet in Your Hectic Life

Designate a cozy chair as your very own. When you need a time-out, take a seat for a few moments of peace and quiet. Everyone knows you can't talk to someone who is in time-out.

Wake up thirty minutes before other family members to start each day as your very own. Savor a warm cup of coffee. Watch the sunrise. Take a quiet walk without an iPod or a friend. Pray. Or read the paper without interruption.

Stay up thirty minutes past other family members to end each day as your very own. Write in your gratitude journal. Say a prayer of thanks. Take a hot bubble bath. Read a book. Or just sit and reflect on your happy day.

Choose a quaint corner of your yard or a sunny spot in the house to grow fresh herbs or flowers. Take time each day to tend to these while focusing on nothing but how much you enjoy their beauty.

If your children cool down with a thirty-minute television show, take that time for yourself. Write a letter to a friend. Organize family photos. Or rearrange the furniture. Do something uplifting for yourself.

Just like that night of grief several months before, as I went back to bed that December night, I knew that I was full—full of the love God has for me. Full, because instead of fighting the quiet, I gave in to it, both as myself before God and as a mother with my children. I did not resist their interruption of my alone time but accepted, as a gift, their desire to be with me. I came seeking, and I received not one but two blessings—the gifts of quiet with my children and quiet with my heavenly Father.

Growing . . . Every Day

There remains no doubt that as mothers, we'll face challenges that will force us to grow and adapt. And while we can certainly glean new understanding by simply reacting to stretching situations, the learning becomes that much richer if we go about our mothering with the intention of growing. Seek out new ways to stretch yourself. Enroll in courses that increase your skills or perhaps even reveal ones you never knew you had. Instead of feeling down on yourself when you fall, pick yourself up, dust yourself off, and strive for a different outcome next time.

Our mothering season doesn't have to be one focused wholly on who we help our children become. In fact, it shouldn't be that narrow at all. Recognize this journey as one that shapes and defines you, helps you scale new heights, and brings you closer to your amazing potential. There is actually a lot of miraculous work going on during this adventure. You're growing, stretching, changing. Just imagine how you'll look at journey's end!

Stretching and Training

1. When was the last time you tried something new?
2. Are there parts of your pre-children life that you left by the wayside when you became a mom? How could you incorporate any of them into your life now in a way that enriches your growth?
3. Is there an area in your life where you feel pulled to make a change? What would that look like, and what

the mommy diaries

practical steps can you take right now to begin to make it happen?

4. Is there a mistake in your past you've been covered in guilt over? How could you begin to let it go in order to move on and become the woman God's created you to be?

5. Think about the growth you've already undergone in the midst of your mothering. Take some time to catalogue how it's made you the fuller, more amazing woman you are today.

3   Relationships
Finding Climbing Partners

Trips into the backcountry aren't meant to be solo expeditions. Mountain climbers rely on their partners for safety as much as encouragement. Setting up and breaking down camps can be an exhausting job—one best suited for a team. And friendly company not only increases the beauty of breathtaking sights on a hike but also protects against veering off the trail and becoming stranded in the wilderness.

Stories of lost hikers often begin with someone getting separated from her partners or starting out on her own to begin with. Such wilderness adventures are designed for teamwork. So too is motherhood. When we try to go it alone and cut ourselves off from the community around us, we often fail. Severe solitude and lack of accountability, support, and sheer understanding leave us stranded without the proper resources to navigate the road in front of us.

Building and investing in relationships during this season of our lives makes us not only better mothers but also better women. Friends help shape us into the women we were designed to be. They laugh with us over a good story, weep when our dreams remain unfulfilled, and challenge us when we're ready to give up. They become necessities for the journey, protecting not only our health, sanity, and sense of perspective but also our ability to fully enjoy the path marked out for us. Who are your climbing partners?

Let's Play Friends
by Rebecca K. Grosenbach

On my daughter Kate's first day of kindergarten, she walked up to a little girl and said, "Hi. My name is Kate. What's yours?"

I was struck by my daughter's ease in making friends. It's too bad most of us outgrow that. I'm usually uncomfortable around people I don't know. I have to force myself to walk up and say, "I don't believe we've met. My name is Becky"— which is, in fact, just a grown-up way of saying what Kate said in kindergarten.

I learned more about making friends when I helped in the "Twos and Threes" class during church. It included lots of hair bows and patent leather shoes and miniature vests and ties. The group scored very high on the cuteness scale.

We played with toys (I got to play trucks), rolled and cut Play-Doh, sang "The B-I-B-L-E," and listened to a Bible story. Our teacher told us about a baby named Moses.

After the story we had snacks. What a great idea. Why don't they serve snacks in "big" church? Then we got to go play in the gym. Another great idea. One little gem of a girl, Tess, asked me to play "friends."

"How do you play 'friends'?" I asked her.

With a little flip of her hand and a cock of her head she said, "Oh, you just talk and stuff."

Then she took my hand, and we started to walk around the gym. Knowing that conversation was key to the success of the game, I tried to get things rolling.

"What's your favorite animal?" I asked her.

"Monkey."

"What's your favorite color?"

"Let's skip."

So we did. And then we ran. When we arrived at the far wall of the gym, Tess proclaimed, "This is my house." Since we were friends, it was only natural she'd take me to her house. Then we ran across the gym to the other wall and arrived at my house. Naturally.

All too soon gym time was over. We had to put away the toys and wait for our moms and dads to come get us.

In the years to come, Tess won't remember playing "friends" with me, but I have a feeling I'll never forget it. She taught me that friends "talk and stuff," hold hands, run, skip, and go to each others' houses. Friendship requires a little bit of time and effort. But that's how the game is played. And everybody who plays, wins.

Friendship is born at that moment when one person says to another, "What! You too? I thought I was the only one."

—C. S. Lewis

Making an Impact
by Michelle Ottoes

One steamy summer night in south Texas, I was with a bunch of women's ministry leaders at a

the mommy diaries

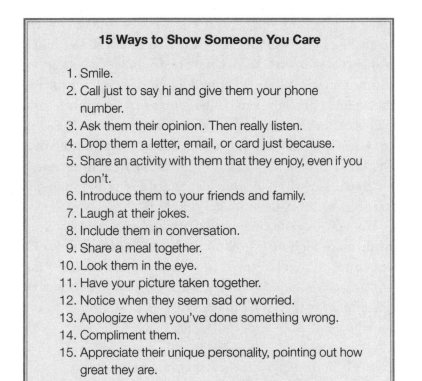

15 Ways to Show Someone You Care

1. Smile.
2. Call just to say hi and give them your phone number.
3. Ask them their opinion. Then really listen.
4. Drop them a letter, email, or card just because.
5. Share an activity with them that they enjoy, even if you don't.
6. Introduce them to your friends and family.
7. Laugh at their jokes.
8. Include them in conversation.
9. Share a meal together.
10. Look them in the eye.
11. Have your picture taken together.
12. Notice when they seem sad or worried.
13. Apologize when you've done something wrong.
14. Compliment them.
15. Appreciate their unique personality, pointing out how great they are.

riverside restaurant as part of a training retreat. I didn't know many of the other ladies very well, but I was relishing the opportunity to have fellowship with other women in the same season of life as me. Accompanying me was my eight-week-old daughter, who was part of the group because she was nursing. After dinner, a few of us went to the bathroom, where I planned to change Emily.

The bathroom was outside and quite rustic. It was also very crowded. The floors and walls were stone, and I experienced a moment of panic as I came to the realization that there was no baby changing table and no countertop to use as a substitute. I turned to the gal behind me, a woman whom

I had just met that night, and said, "I guess the only place to change Emily's diaper is on the floor, but I wish I had a blanket to lay down first." Without one moment of hesitation, this mom took off her shirt and laid it on the floor for me to lay Emily on. She even balled it up a little at the top for a pillow. After I got over my embarrassment at not thinking to take off my own shirt, I grew more and more amazed that she stood there in her bra among all those other women and chatted easily with me while I changed Emily and then put her shirt back on like it was no big deal.

For her to sacrifice her modesty to serve me and my child really made an impression on me, and it is an example of a very important truth that I have learned from connecting with other moms. As moms, we are called to serve each other in ways that don't make sense or mean much to the outside world but mean *everything* to us.

Mom's Theater
by Barbara Vogelgesang

For six months I played with the idea of starting a theater company, but I kept wondering if I could do it. I discussed it with my friend Mary as we sat waiting for our daughters' ballet class to end. I hadn't been involved in any theatrical productions for years and years, and my confidence level was pretty low. She encouraged me and offered to help in whatever way she could. She sensed my insecurity and promised to pray.

I love musicals and often played Broadway musical sound-tracks while cleaning the house, singing and dancing for my preschool audience. As the kids grew, they joined me in my "performances." They learned to love reciting great lines and emoting, but could I really take this show on the road? I was just a mom.

"Happy Mother's Day, Mom!" a chorus of voices shouted out as each of my four children laid a small envelope in front of me. I had expected the usual gifts of homemade pictures, flowers, and chocolate. This was different. The kids looked nervous as they encouraged me to open their envelopes. I glanced at my husband, looking for some insight, but he just grinned from ear to ear. I opened the envelopes. Loose change fell out of the envelope from my five-year-old. "It's a $1.87. I've been saving up," he proudly announced. I found crumpled dollars and change in the next gift from my six-year-old. When I opened the envelopes from my teens, they each contained $20 with notes that read, "We believe in you and want to be the first investors in your theater company." I sat there with tears in my eyes. My family thought I could do this. I didn't know how, but that didn't seem to matter—they still had faith in me.

The pressure of living up to my family's expectations now weighed upon me. I thought about it constantly as I went through my usual mom duties that next week. Trudging into the library with our weekly load of books, I thought, "How and where am I going to do this?" The kids scattered to their favorite bookracks, and I sat down in one of the library chairs to think and make notes.

"So, I hear you are starting a theater company here in town," the librarian's cheerful voice rang out. Donna and I were friends and often discussed children's books and events at the library for the kids. Obviously the kids had mentioned my idea. "The movie theater has a new owner, and she would love to have a theater company call that place home. Can I give her your number?" I sat there thrilled and amazed. This was going to happen. "Let me know if I can help with anything," the librarian offered. A mom sitting nearby overheard our conversation and handed me a piece of paper, saying, "Oh, my kids would love to do theater. Please put us on your mailing list and I'll help too."

A few days later the owner of the theater, Barbara, called me. "What days do you need the theater for auditions, rehearsals, and the show? I want to put it on my calendar." I asked her what the cost of renting the theater would be. "I just want the theater filled with kids. Providing that for them is payment enough," she said. I felt myself being pulled along on this incredible adventure.

A few weeks later, I found myself conducting auditions for my first show. I was overwhelmed at the number of kids who came. I gave myself one month to put on the production. My dear friend Mary sat beside me as my codirector. I didn't have the heart to turn any of these young performers away, so I wrote new parts into our show. They were all so delighted when I called them that night to tell them their role.

The next month was intense but incredible. The kids worked hard and had so much fun. They each sold a handful of tickets, so I knew we would have a small audience. I was hoping to be able to pay the few bills we had and provide a pizza party between shows.

On performance day, Mary and I got to the theater early to make sure everything was ready. I was still hoping we would get a decent audience. I had asked a mom and Barbara to take care of any walk-up ticket sales while we were busy

the mommy diaries

in the auditorium. Barbara and my husband came down the aisle and asked me to step into the lobby for a minute. Worried, I opened the door to find the lobby filled with people. There was my husband's grin again. He kissed me and whispered, "I knew you could do it."

The kids did an amazing job, and the show was a complete success. Now I'm not "Ms. Director" or even "Mrs. V" to thirty theater-crazy kids; I'm just "Theater Mom." I can't wait for the next production.

> You can learn many things from children. How much patience you have, for instance.
> —Franklin P. Jones

Winning Relationships
by Jami Kirkbride

"I'm a winner! I'm a winner!" he squealed with delight. Jackson came running toward me as I sat outside the mall arcade enjoying an Italian soda with my husband. His tiny little frame bobbed up and down as he tried to skip toward us. His sparkling eyes and chubby cheeks glowed with enthusiasm, and his arms waved widely in the air. When he reached me he threw his arms around me and gave me a giant hug.

"Good job! You are a winner," I smiled and planted a kiss on the tip of his button nose.

"I'm . . . I'm . . . I'm . . . I'm gonna go do it again," he stuttered with excitement, and he scooted along.

From the table where we were sitting, we could see our three-year-old son, Jackson, as he played just inside the door of the mall arcade. He didn't have any tokens, and the games weren't really even working, but as he moved the levers, knobs, and buttons, his confidence grew. He thought he was not just really playing but really winning. He laughed, talked to himself, and jumped up and down with joy. This was a side of Jackson we rarely saw. My husband and I sat amazed at the fun Jackson was having. He never asked for tokens or seemed worried about the other boys. He just thoroughly enjoyed what he was doing.

"Isn't it interesting to see the difference in Jackson's demeanor and personality when he's apart from his brothers?" I asked my husband. "He just seems more outgoing and confident," I noted. "His personality seems a little brighter." He played well with his brothers and little sister and loved them a lot. He was happy and talkative, but he was just different on his own.

"What are we supposed to do about that?" my husband asked. "It's not like his brothers are going anywhere." We both laughed. As parents of four, we often discussed our children's unique personalities and individual needs. We knew we wouldn't be able to parent perfectly but didn't want to overlook things just because there were four of them.

Later that night as I was showering, I replayed the whole scenario in my mind. It had been refreshing and fun to watch Jackson. He had been so enthusiastic and confident. We often saw his cautious and reserved side. He wasn't typically bold, loud, or self-assured. But seeing him skip about, arms in the air, had done something for my own soul. Something in me longed for that same confidence and freedom of expression.

I began to reflect on my own life and some relationships that surrounded me. A couple of my friendships were

the mommy diaries

discouraging me. I was feeling hampered and stifled, struggling to be myself and feel accepted that way. I would often end up feeling as though I were inferior or incapable. Relationships can be a challenge. For a number of years I had been frustrated with friendships with women. They could be so rewarding and yet so tricky. I started to take inventory of how my relationships were affecting me and the person I was becoming.

It was quite eye-opening to realize that I had a couple friendships in my life that were not very healthy. I needed to take some time and space away from those in order to get myself on track. I wasn't being the person God had created me to be. I had fallen into a pattern of trying to be everything others wanted from me. Yet I would still walk away feeling as though I wasn't enough. I realized that just as Jackson needed some space and room to express himself and grow, I needed that too. I had become distracted by trying to figure out the games some women play and how to avoid the pitfalls. I felt drained and spent. Just as Jackson's siblings would still be around, my friends would be also. What I needed was some space to form friendships that would encourage me to be all God wanted from me. I wasn't going to be much good to God if I remained stifled and felt useless. I needed to foster relationships that would help me feel valued, able, and energetic as I faced the adventures ahead.

> So encourage each other and build each other up.
> 1 Thessalonians 5:11 NLT

I also needed some of that good one-on-one time with the One who created me. I would get my refreshment, confidence, and worth from him. I hadn't realized what my soul was longing for until I saw the vivid image of Jackson. Since that day I have tried to become more aware of the relationships that surround me. Are they serving as a form of encouragement or distraction as I pursue God's plan? Do my relationships encourage me to see myself as God sees me? In his eyes I'm a winner!

The Mom in the Mirror
by Karen Ehman

I'll never forget the day I saw myself in that mirror. Even though over a decade of time has passed since I caught the glimpse, the image is still vivid. And I'm sorry to say that it wasn't a pretty one. My then six-year-old daughter and her three-year-old brother were playing together in their room. I strolled down the hall to check on the baby, who was due up from his nap soon.

As I approached the room where my kids were playing, I heard Mackenzie's voice pipe up as she expressed to Mitchell her immense displeasure. You see, he was not stacking the colorful, snap-together, plastic blocks in an organized manner that suited her fancy. As I neared the door I heard her sharply declare, "No, Mitchell. Not *that* way! Oh . . . just give it to me! Everybody knows they go like *this*, not like *that*. Can't you ever do anything right?" Her words, though unkind, weren't the real issue. What bothered me most was that they were spoken in a caustic, condescending tone. I was not going to let her get away with that.

I stepped into the room and in classic mom form—hand on hip, finger pointed, throwing the child's middle name in for emphasis—I gave it to her. "Mackenzie Leith Ehman!

Young lady, I don't *ever* want to hear you talk to your brother like that again!"

The lingering image of what happened next is forever seared in my mind. My little princess didn't defend her actions. She didn't let out the proverbial "But *Mommy, he* started it." Oh, no. Without even looking up from her pile of blocks, she calmly and very matter-of-factly retorted, "Why not, Mama? You talk like that to Daddy all the time."

My heart instantaneously sank and broke at the same time. As often is the case, children serve as a painstakingly honest mirror when it comes to our attitudes and actions as mothers. The offense my daughter had committed that day paled in comparison to what I suddenly feared my kids were witnessing in our home as they saw their mom interact with their dad in a disrespectful manner. The oft-quoted adage is excruciatingly true: "More is caught than is taught." I can orally instruct my kids to speak respectfully to others at all times. However, that verbal life lesson goes right out the window when they see me belittle my husband, even though at times it is cleverly cloaked in humor.

Horrified at my daughter's response, I shed a tear. Then I whispered a heartfelt and committed prayer. I knew I had to take action. Ashamedly, I told my husband what had transpired. Later that day, I bared my soul to my moms' group. Turns out I wasn't the only woman who had a little mirror or two in her house. Many of my colleagues in the school of mothering had also seen themselves vividly reflected through the voices and actions of their offspring. We vowed together to keep our words and tones in check. Of course, we found out this is often easier said than done.

Having a friend in whom you can confide helps—one who knows that your heart's desire is to model for your children verbal respect, not only to your husband but to the policeman, the grocery store clerk, your mother-in-law, and even complete strangers. Forging a friendship based on encouragement and accountability in this area can be just the catalyst for keeping your tongue in check while you have little eyes riveted firmly upon you.

Lest we be discouraged, the reflections we spy in our little ones aren't always unpleasant. God often gives us glimpses of glory in our little mirrors too. A soft, downy head bowed seriously in bedtime prayer, bringing petitions on behalf of a sick classmate "because you always pray for sick friends, Mommy." A toddler's chubby fingers digging deep into their coat pocket on a chilly December day, searching for a coin or two to drop in the red bucket at the department store, as he says, "You don't ever walk by that man without giving him money, Mom. Maybe we should go buy him a hot chocolate too. That would make him happy." Yes, the mommy mirror reflects all images, both the good and the not-so-lovely. May our aim be to present to those sponges residing under our roof an accurate picture of God. To model for them words of life and hope, the kind that build up rather than tear down. Pretty, shiny, sparkling mirrors. Not the dingy, dirty sort.

> Children in a family are like flowers in a bouquet: there's always one determined to face in an opposite direction from the way the arranger desires.
> —Marcelene Cox

A long time has passed since I spied my ugly self in the mirror that day. I still struggle at times with a sharp tongue, often saying things in jest that in reality are unkind. And my kids now reserve the right to call me on the carpet for such behavior. We moms need to continually remind ourselves that there are little and not so little eyes watching and in many cases imitating what they see. What's in your mirror?

Mothering Guides
by Barbara Vogelgesang

When I was expecting my first child, I read every book on the market. I wanted to be the best, most informed mother I could be. My own mom lived two states away, and I was determined to do this on my own. Little did I know that I'd had mothering guides from the day I was born; I just never noticed. It wasn't until I was in the midst of raising my children that I realized the impact those women had on me.

I know our mothers are undeniably the first to influence the mothers each of us will become. My mom taught me to serve my family and gave me an example of strength to persevere through any struggle. I learned from her example what kind of mother I wanted my children to have.

The other women in my family also left their mark on the mother I became. My grandmothers differed not only in their nationalities but also in their styles. I remember Grandma Collum with her boisterous Irish laughter. She was always leading me in some hilarious game. She loved having people around and throwing a good party. If we had a bottle of soda, some chips, and music, we had the makings of a good time. My Italian grandmother, Grandma Minerva, taught me to sew, grow my own tomatoes, and cook the most delicious meals. I fondly remember lunch in her little garden in Brooklyn. I thought it was the most peaceful place in New York. As a mom, I now enjoy teaching my own girls how to cook, sew, and enjoy the peace of the garden. I also can put together a good time with minimal preparation, and I am always ready for a good laugh.

I also had quite a varied group of aunts from whom to glean. Aunt Grace, my workplace aunt, taught me that a woman could be successful in the business world and taught me the importance of an education. Aunt Ann demonstrated a loyalty to family and tradition that was unshakable. My Aunt Jean taught me that God brings a family together in different ways. She fiercely loved my two adopted cousins and gave every bit of herself to them.

When I got married and joined my husband on the Ringling Bros. Circus, I found mothering guides from all over the world. I learned the importance of passing on special skills and cultural customs, having a family team, and working together. I absorbed the different ways families loved and enjoyed each other.

As our family grew, I became more aware of the mothering guides in my life and that I am not doing and cannot do this mothering thing alone. I needed support from women who have been there, done that and women who were in the trenches alongside me and women who hadn't even begun the adventure.

I must admit that some mothers influenced me because the way they handled things illustrated what not to do. They also made me realize what was really important to me. A friend from college visited us with her two children

the mommy diaries

for a weekend. My nerves were shot by the time they went home. They didn't really do anything terrible. I was just used to my style of parenting, which was much quieter. It is important to me that we sit down to a peaceful meal. This friend and her husband didn't mind if their kids did laps around the table as long as they finished their green beans. I wanted my kids to have their napkins on their laps. We had different styles, and it made me aware of what was important to me.

Some of the training I got was from positive role models like my friend Sally, who is ever gracious and generous. She taught me to think about the impact each of my decisions will make in my children's future and to pray unceasingly.

> You can kiss your family and friends good-bye and put miles between you, but at the same time you carry them with you in your heart, your mind, your stomach, because you do not just live in a world but a world lives in you.
>
> —Frederick Buechner

"Marty, Libby just drank a whole bottle of baby Tylenol," I cried to one of the mentors God put in my life when my daughter was two years old. "I'm the worst mom ever." I was on the phone and hysterical. I had already called the doctor, who had told me my little girl would be fine, but I needed to be reassured by a mom whose children had lived through their toddler years. "She will be fine," Marty comforted me. "We've all got a story like this. Let me tell you about when. . . ." Many other women like Marty also shared their own mothering struggles and gave me hope in the middle of a crisis.

I'm so grateful now that I don't travel this road alone. I look for the guides now, instead of struggling unnecessarily.

I also find that I am a guide for those who are coming after me. It's an exciting adventure, isn't it?

A Two-Way Street
by Laura Broadwater

My youngest son and I were on our way home from running errands one day when he suddenly leaned over and placed his head against my shoulder. I glanced down at him. He seemed to be doing this a lot lately, and it worried me. This behavior was unusual for him. Having an older brother who thought being the oldest came with the inherent rights of "boss and bully," my youngest usually expended much energy acting tough and standing his ground. But we were alone, and I figured that maybe he thought it was safe to let down his guard. Still, careful not to make him feel like a baby, I playfully asked, "What ya doing?"

"Getting."

Curious about such an odd response, I asked, "What are you getting?"

"Love," he replied.

"Oh," I smiled, nodding my head. And for the rest of the ride home, he remained in that position.

The next time we were out driving and he did it, I casually asked, "Are you needing some love?" His answer surprised me.

"No, Mom, I'm giving it."

Shocked, I drove on in silence, pondering the wisdom of his words—and the simple fact that I might need love too. I was so used to giving love to those around me who were in

the mommy diaries

need of it that I'd never thought about receiving it myself. Not even from God.

This practice continued on between us for years. After a while, though, I stopped asking whether he was "getting" or "giving." The mere action itself served as a reminder of the need for balance in my life when it came to the giving and receiving of love.

With much regret, the day finally came when we had to abandon this practice. He just got too big (even when scrunched down) to lean his head on my shoulder. Still, regardless of how tall or grown up he gets, I won't forget the lesson he taught me while out driving down those country roads: loving someone is meant to be a two-way street.

> Piglet sidled up to Pooh from behind. "Pooh!" he whispered. "Yes, Piglet?" "Nothing," said Piglet, taking Pooh's paw. "I just wanted to be sure of you."
> —A. A. Milne

Gummy Gifts

by Amy Nappa

As the mother of a boy, I've often envied those with girls— all those adorable clothes! Frilly dresses, ribbons and bows, and lots and lots of shoes. But at my house it was a regular uniform of a T-shirt, sweatpants, and snow boots. Yes, snow boots. For nearly one whole year, no matter what the weather, my preschooler, Tony, wore snow boots. In his mind, they became a key part of any costume he imagined. They were pirate boots, cowboy boots, space ranger boots. They were easy to slip off and on and made great stomping noises. Snow boots.

One day Tony came home from playing with a friend. He smiled his precious smile as I welcomed him in the door. "Did you have fun?" I asked.

"Yep. And we had a good snack too. I saved you some," he answered. Even as my lips were saying, "How nice of you!" my mind was quickly thinking, "Your hands are empty and those sweatpants don't have any pockets . . . so where is this snack?" Before I could voice this thought, Tony took off one of those snow boots, reached inside, and pulled out a handful of sock-lint-covered gummy bears. He proudly offered them to me.

I did what any mother worth her salt would do: I ate them. Every last one. I hugged Tony and thanked him for his thoughtfulness. He seemed satisfied that I'd enjoyed his gift and sauntered off to play. It was only then that I wiped the lint off of my tongue.

Most people laugh when I tell them this story. In fact, it's one of the only "mom" stories that Tony, who is grown and will be leaving for college soon, allows me to tell in front of his friends. It does reveal a little about the kind of mother I am—not so worried about germs, encouraging jumping on the beds, and serving ice cream for breakfast. But it really tells more about Tony. He's thoughtful.

I tend to be a person who has good intentions. I *think* about sending a note. *Intend* to call a friend. See a cute craft in a magazine and *imagine* myself making that for a girlfriend. But I often get busy and put those things off. I excuse my poor behavior by saying, "She's busy too. . . . She won't mind that I didn't write . . . call . . . surprise her with a gift." I think my efforts at the friendship might not matter that much to someone else. But I'm just kidding myself. All those thoughtful gestures *do* matter.

If a mom will gladly receive (and eat!) a damp and fuzzy handful of candies direct from the toe of a sweaty snow boot, a friend would gladly welcome a thoughtful gesture from me. The little things do matter, even if they're not elaborate or expensive. My perspective changed a bit because of Tony's gift. Other people don't magically know I'm thinking about them or that I love them. I need to let them know. So do you.

Perfect Strangers

by Tally Flint

About a year ago, a woman touched my life in ways no one else ever had before. Through her story I not only learned more about myself but also changed the way I view my world. Because our paths crossed, I am a different woman, and the funny thing is, I never even actually met her. Our relationship began with her death and the legacy she left behind.

On a cold November night, a friend called to say that one of the moms from our MOPS group had been involved in a hit-and-run accident. I listened in numb shock as the caller shared how the family of four had been crossing a downtown street when a drunk driver ran a red light and plowed into them, killing the mom and toddlers and injuring the father. They'd been out enjoying one of their family traditions: riding downtown on the light rail to get hot cocoa from their favorite café. The two kids, snuggled in the stroller, were dressed up in their treasured outfits: a princess gown for the four-year-old daughter and a Superman cape for the two-year-old son.

I racked my brain for any recollection of this mom and came up empty-handed. Try as I might, I could not place her. Even days later, once the news stations had plastered photos of the family on the television screens of homes around the city, I still didn't recognize the smiling face that stared out at me. We'd only been having MOPS meetings for a few weeks at this point, and it was obvious that since Becca wasn't in my discussion group, our paths just hadn't crossed. I felt no connection to the *woman*, but as I began to process the tragedy, I felt a deep bond with the *mom*. The next few MOPS meetings morphed from the planned speakers the steering committee had arranged the previous summer to impromptu memorial services and grief counseling sessions.

I was surprised to find that I wasn't the only one who'd never met Becca. It seemed many of our moms never knew her but were struggling with the same overwhelming grief I was feeling at the loss of her life and the lives of her children. Like her, we had children of our own, we visited our own local hot spots, we walked those same downtown streets. As I listened to the stories women shared of how Becca's life had touched them both before and after her death, I began to paint a picture of the kind of person she was—the kind of mother she was.

Everyone remarked on how creative and imaginative Becca was with her kids. They told of impromptu face-painting sessions, costume parties, and good old-fashioned fun. It seemed she was a mom who celebrated her daughter's love for all things princess and her son's infatuation with super-heroism. She was the kind of mom who sang silly songs, played without worrying about making a mess, and didn't hesitate to make a special outing for a delicious cup of hot cocoa.

Weeks turned into months and I still found myself thinking of Becca. When my infant daughter woke up crying for the fourth time that night, I stopped myself short of resenting her when I remembered the loss of Becca. My son's defiant attitude still irked me, but my anger fizzled when I realized the joy it was to walk alongside him and discover the strong-willed young man he'd

> Light tomorrow
> with today!
> —Elizabeth Barrett Browning

someday become. I let go of my reservations and got dirty with my kids again. I stopped caring about spilled milk or how fast we could load up into the car. I decided to embrace life again, because as Becca reminded me daily, I had no idea how long it'd be mine to enjoy.

I may never have met her face-to-face, but Becca has become the perfect stranger for me. She's touched my life in ways she might never have if we'd actually met. And the beauty of her legacy has left me wondering what sort of legacy I'm creating for my own family. I want it to be one of fun, laughter, joy, and faith. And with Becca's influence, it is becoming just that.

The Power of Human Touch
by Leslie Parrott

I've been pregnant twice, and both times it was difficult, to say the least—especially on the first round. Because of complications that were not entirely clear, I was ordered by my doctor to remain on round-the-clock bed rest just three months into my first pregnancy. I could only leave the house for medical appointments, and I was to remain on my left side as much as possible.

Six months into the pregnancy, the doctor decided to place me in the hospital. "I'm not sure what's happening," the doctor told me, "but from the sonogram we can see that your baby isn't getting the nutrition he needs. He's not growing."

With my life at serious risk, our baby boy, John, was born two weeks later, February 8, through emergency C-section. He was three months premature and weighed just over a pound. Rushed into the neonatal intensive care unit, John was attached to monitors and machines that helped him breathe, regulate his temperature, and do everything else a tiny body must do to live.

the mommy diaries

It was almost more than a mother could bear to see his tiny frame barely hanging on to life. We didn't know if he would make it, and more than one doctor suggested we prepare for the worst. We prayed desperately for this baby.

A week later, the phone woke us out of a restless sleep. It was John's primary nurse calling to tell us that our newborn son was going into emergency surgery. We raced to the hospital just in time to see his one-pound body being wheeled down the corridor of the hospital on an adult-sized gurney surrounded by two surgeons and four technicians.

I've never prayed more intensely, cried more deeply, or agonized more severely. I called every prayer warrior I could think of to pray with us. I couldn't bear the thought of losing this child, yet I knew it was a strong possibility.

The surgery lasted nearly three hours, but it seemed like three days. Finally the chief surgeon walked into the waiting room to give us the news. His face gave me no clue as to the condition of my child. I held my husband's hand so tightly I'm surprised I didn't break a bone. The doctor sat down on the edge of the coffee table facing us to tell us that Baby John's abdominal surgery was successful.

For the next three months Baby John lay in his isolette in the ICU. And every day we sat by his side in our sterile gowns as the machines around him hummed and beeped. Then one day his nurse, Margaret, quietly asked me if I'd like to hold John in my own arms for ten minutes.

His little life was ten days old, you see, and I hadn't been able to hold him because as a micro-preemie, his body couldn't withstand the stimulation. So when Margaret asked, I immediately teared up.

She took blankets out of the warming oven, bundled him up, and placed him in my arms with tubes and wires still attached to his body. I held him for just ten minutes, but Margaret had no idea what a difference this made for me. She also had no idea that it happened to be my birthday. And it was the best gift I've ever received.

To this day, seven years later, I still cherish that moment. And recently, while traveling in Colorado where Margaret now lives, I went out of my way to thank her again. "Do you have any idea what you did for me that day you let me hold John for the first time?" I asked her.

"I'm so glad I could do that for you," she replied.

"It made all the difference in the world to me," I told her. And it did. Margaret didn't have to do that. If fact, she went to extraordinary lengths to maneuver the machinery and everything else for me. Holding John was a turning point.

The next day, as he rested in his plastic isolette, we were allowed to put our hands through its small portals and gently contain him with one hand on his head and the other around his feet. Then Margaret and one of the doctors explained to us the value of something they called "kangaroo care." This is the tender act of holding a preemie against your chest, skin-on-skin, for a few minutes each day. What a difference that made!

> There is no better way to thank God for your sight than by giving a helping hand to someone in the dark.
>
> —Helen Keller

It made a difference not just for us, as parents getting to revel in holding this little life that we feared we might lose, but for John. As he grew accustomed to our touch, we learned more about the importance of touching him. With a university library at our disposal,

the mommy diaries

we researched how we could help our son make progress. And our studies brought us to a conviction we hold even more firmly today: there is power in human touch.

Just as holding John that first time did wonders for my heart and soul, our gentle caresses brought new life to his tiny body. And even today, we use human touch to soothe, encourage, and even restore our most important relationships.

Midnight Kisses
by Elsa Kok Colopy

They didn't have to open their home to me. My big brother had a family of his own—a beautiful wife, three preschoolers. I was a young single mom with a broken past. Why add to their already full brood? But they did. They threw the door wide and invited my three-year-old and me to live with them until I could get on my feet.

I got a job at a local restaurant. The money was good, and I could spend most of the day with my daughter. But it meant late nights, sometimes very late nights if I had to close. Carol, my sister-in-law, cared for my daughter on those late evenings—tucking her in bed, reading her stories, praying with her.

One evening I came in late and saw something on the kitchen table. I crept closer and smiled as I recognized it. Two chocolate kisses atop a note. I read the words, "Roses are red, violets are blue; this chocolate, my sis, is just for you. Love, Carol." I grinned from ear to ear and popped the chocolate into my mouth. As I savored the sweet flavor, I pulled out a pen and flipped her paper over. "Roses are red," I wrote, "grass is green, this chocolate, my sis, was mighty keen!"

On that late Friday night, a tradition was born. Each and every night I'd find a poem and two chocolate kisses. I'd write back and tell her, in rhyme form, all about my day. "People were cold, not nice at all; work was a bust, I'm about to bawl" or "Big tips tonight, sweet friend and sis, so I'm especially loving this yummy midnight kiss!"

During the day my daughter and I witnessed a family that worked. Mom, dad, three little ones. I watched as they lovingly disciplined, taught, and adventured with their kids. I giggled as they laughed, teased, and chased each other for tickle fests. They included my girl in all they did, and she reveled in the love and laughter. Nightly sleepovers with her cousins became her own chocolate kisses, sweet to savor and wrapped in love.

I suppose my brother could have worried about my broken history. He could have protected his kids from our wounded influence. I would have understood if he turned away the two extra mouths to feed. He was a pastor, so it wasn't as though he had extra money to toss around. But he didn't turn me away; he welcomed me in. He and his wife gave me a six-month window to earn some money and find a place. They offered me shelter in the storm, a haven, chocolate kisses, and rhyming love notes.

On one of my last days before moving into my own place, I penned a final poem for my sister-in-love:

> Chocolate kisses you've given, warm meals at night;
> You scooped us up from our heartbreaking plight.
> I saw Jesus in you, and it's changed how I live.
> You gave us love, all you had to give:

Hugs to my girl, tucking her into her bed,
Praying over her as she bowed her head,
Including your children as you served our need,
Teaching and loving, planting those seeds.
I only hope someday, I grow to be like you,
Living and loving Jesus in all that I do.

Years have gone by since my brother's family took me in.
But I haven't forgotten the powerful lesson their love introduced to my world. And it was a family affair. Their kids
made welcome signs when we first moved in. They shared
their room with my daughter. They invited her to play with
their friends. They enveloped us in their world. As a family,
they impacted our messy lives with grace and generosity.
And I am forever grateful.

Needing Others . . . Every Day

Relationships have their season just like anything else.
Some last a lifetime, growing and stretching right alongside
us. Others step in for a time of need, leave an impact, and
drift away again, never to return. Some explore the intimate
crevices of our personhood; others merely scratch the surface. But all, regardless of the forms they take, play a role in
our development and maturation as women.

This journey set before us isn't meant to be traveled alone.
The lessons prove richer, the learning deeper, the joy more
pleasurable, the fears and tragedies less threatening, when
we walk alongside others who care for us and understand
where we've been and where we're headed. Take the time to
cultivate a support system. Invest in the lives God's placed

alongside you. Reach out to them as they reach out to you. Experience your adventure to the fullest.

Finding Your Climbing Partners

1. Can you point to key relationships in your life that pour into you and your personal journey as a mother?
2. What differences have they made in your experience?
3. Are there places in your life where you feel you're stranded, navigating the path alone?
4. What forms of support could you really use in these areas to help you flourish instead of merely survive?
5. Are you preventing yourself from creating healthy, caring relationships by holding back parts of yourself?
6. What do you need to let go of in order to begin flourishing in your relationships?

4   Help
Utilizing Guidebooks and Gear

Tune in to any sportscaster's postgame interview show and you'll hear a similar message in every player's comments. It's one of teamwork, camaraderie, and pooling resources to get the job done. No one seems to claim credit for a win all by himself. In fact, in cycling's most prestigious race, the Tour de France, teammates actually draft off one another to ensure a win for their best cyclist.

Unfortunately, society's view of motherhood doesn't embrace such an open acknowledgment that everyone needs help. The unspoken assumption is that we will do it all—all on our own. Excel in a career, raise caring and intelligent children, thrive as a supportive spouse, and make the world a better place—all in a day's work for a mother. We've come to see asking for help as a sign of weakness. And when we do grow desperate enough to ask for it, guilt attacks us for daring to impose on someone else's life. We frantically think of ways we can immediately repay the favor. No one wants to be indebted.

> Two are better than one,
>   because they have a good
>   return for their work:
> If one falls down,
>   his friend can help him up.
> But pity the man who falls
>   and has no one to help him up!
>
>   Ecclesiastes 4:9–10

Ironically enough, we are all already indebted. All we have become as women, the gifts and talents we call our own, and the circumstances that have moved us through our journey have all been gifts of some sort or another. Family members invested in our development, society supported our education, and benevolent strangers made an impact on our lives. As humans, and especially as mothers, we need help. We cannot do it alone, and isn't it time we realized no one really expects us to? Here's to learning to be dependent.

Help Wanted
by Tally Flint

Asking for help does not come naturally to me. It's a pride thing. If I were to seek assistance from someone else, I'd be admitting I couldn't handle it on my own. People would find out I don't always have it all together—that I don't actually know what I'm doing half the time.

When my son was born, I worked full time and went to grad classes once a week to finish my master's degree. I wanted to breastfeed, so I lugged my Medela Pump In Style to and from work everyday and stayed up late each night readying it for the next day. Sterilized parts? Check.

Full stash of freezer bags? Check. Ice pack frozen? Check. I'd wake up at 5:00 a.m. every day just so I could get myself ready, nurse my son, and get us out the door on time for our forty-minute commute. Then I'd come home that night and do it all over again.

Sure, I have a lot of warm and endearing memories from that period. But I also remember feeling exhausted. Of all the times to need help, this one was a doozy. And yet I never once asked my husband to clean my pump for me or my friend to watch my son so I could sneak a catnap or some quality study time.

When my daughter was born two and a half years later, I needed help again, and this time I was desperate enough to ask for it. Suddenly I didn't care if the dishes got put back in the wrong place—at least they were clean! And if friends offered to keep bringing me meals even though my daughter was already a month old, I wasn't going to stop them just because I worried they might think I was selfish. Sure, I still had to swallow down the pride and control thing, but those were issues I could deal with later. At the moment I just needed the help!

Mothering is *hard work*. And when you factor in all the other parts of a woman's life (job, spouse, ministry, school, girlfriends, etc.), it gets even harder. I don't think we were meant to do it alone. My church is really big on community, and rarely a Sunday service goes by without someone referring to God's plan for us to live within community. It's a lesson God has really been beating me over the head with lately. He's teaching me that within a body of other faith-seekers, I can know him on a level that would otherwise be unattainable. Likewise, I think we can experience motherhood, and life in general, on a deeper level when we walk alongside and sometimes even in the arms of others. This idea of helping one another—giving and receiving without any strings or expectations attached—captures a glimpse of what the abundant life Jesus talked about is like.

Now I think of learning to ask for help as a spiritual discipline. The more I can give up my pride and open a door for God to work through someone to help me, the more trusting and genuine my relationship with God and those he uses becomes. In becoming vulnerable, I grow closer to him—the whole "he's made perfect in our weaknesses"

the mommy diaries

thing. I can't do it all, and in fact, I was never meant to. It's such a freeing concept.

It's All Up to Me

by Elisa Morgan

I have a bad habit. Like most people with bad habits, I didn't really intend for it to develop. It has gradually grown up in my days without my even noticing. Over time, a layer here, a layer there, its influence increased until I just looked up one morning and voila! There it was for me to see: a bad habit.

If you scanned the surface of my life, you might not notice it. It doesn't really stick out and scream, "Whoa! Stinky bad habit!" It's subtle. Hidden. Tricky for even me to detect at times. What is it? This: thinking life is all up to me. That I'm in charge. That I actually get to choose—for me, of course, and for everybody else too.

I'm stunned when my teenage son prefers the presence of his darling girlfriend to mine. Or I discover that I'm caught off guard when my older-than-teenage daughter doesn't think to ask my opinion when she takes a job. I notice that my husband manages self-discovery without my brilliant psychoanalytic insights. Even the family cats cast only an obligatory glance when I walk in the room. Go figure.

Slowly but surely, over the years of mothering and managing a home and a career and a life, I've made the very wrong assumption that it's all up to me. That it's up to me to make my family a happy family, to control how my children turn out, and for sure to interpret every emotion displayed to everybody within hearing distance. I thought it was my job to explain my son's sarcasm to his father, my husband's anger to his son, and my daughter's outbursts to her brother. I believed it was my fault if husband, son, daughter—and yes, even cats—missed a cue, miscommunicated, or misstepped in their interactions.

As it turns out, I'm wrong. This responsible-for-everybody-and-all-their-feelings-at-all-times thing is a habit that needs to be broken. I know I shouldn't be too hard on myself here. Many bad habits are simply good habits taken too far, stretched beyond their intended purpose. There *was* a time when it fell to me to pick out clothes, select seasonal activities, and interpret my eighteen-month-old's speech to a babysitter. I was schooled by my children's needs toward this habit of helping and handling whatever I could. What would they have done without me? But as my children change, my mothering habits must as well. What worked in the past as a good habit requires redirection now.

> A mother is not a person to lean on, but a person to make leaning unnecessary.
> —Dorothy Fisher

The truth is that it's not all up to me. My job was to steer my children's lives in preparation for them to someday take over. Like training wheels, I was there for them to lean on only until they learned to find other strengths to support themselves.

No, it's not all up to me. It's up to Someone far bigger. With tender redirection, God reveals to me and to my children that in the end, it's up to him. What's left to me? Two things: First, to summon courage to let go and let my children learn this truth themselves. And second, to release control in my own life and consistently remember, yes, it's up to him.

the mommy diaries

My Hero
by Elsa Kok Colopy

She was my hero. The mother of five, Jennifer ran her home like a well-oiled machine. The children, though small, did their chores without complaint. They always used their manners and looked beautiful. The girls had bows and the boys smelled clean nearly all the time.

I was in awe. My one daughter kept me running in circles. More often than not, I had some type of food stain on my shirt, while my girl sported several on her shorts, T-shirts, and face. When Jennifer posted a chore list on her refrigerator, the chores were actually completed. When I posted my list, three weeks later it was forgotten. One more month and we found it underneath the couch. "What happened here?" I asked my girl.

"Don't know, Mama," Sam grinned. "Wanna play hopscotch?"

"Sure!" And off we'd go. I needed help.

It happened in an unexpected way one summer afternoon. Jennifer and I were sitting together on her front porch. I'd been contemplating how I could ask for her help, when Jennifer turned to me. "I need your help," she said.

I looked at her, surprised. "You need my help?"

"Yes," she said. She went on to explain that she felt like she wasn't able to play with her children. "I love how you get down on the floor and play with Sam. I don't know what it is, but I just can't seem to let loose and play like that. How do you do it?"

My jaw dropped. "How do I play? And here I was wondering how I could get your help! I can't get Sam to keep her shirts clean for more than five minutes. And how do I get her to clean her room without having a showdown or a procrastination excuse-fest? How do you do it?"

Jennifer laughed. I laughed.

"I'll teach you how to play," I said, "if you teach me how to actually use a chore list."

"Deal," she smiled. "I'll teach you how to keep clothes clean if you'll teach me how to roll around on the floor and giggle like a wild woman."

We held out our pinky fingers and officially pinky swore on it.

It's nearly ten years later as I write this. I'm better organized because of my sweet friend's influence. She plays more with her five beautiful children. Yes, she still leans toward super-organization, and I still tend to fly (stumble, bump, trip) by the seat of my pants—but we're better for having known each other. More balanced. Better moms. And for that I'm grateful.

Navigating Family Setbacks
by Carla Foote

The headline that morning read "Fed Chief Seeing Signs of Recovery," but economic adversity became personal in our home on a Thursday morning at 10:00 a.m. My husband called me to say that he was being escorted to the door of his office building by a security guard; he could return that evening with the guard to pick up his personal belongings. The high tech sector isn't particularly friendly in their layoff procedures, fearing angry ex-employees who could sabotage

the mommy diaries

a computer system. Even though we had experienced a layoff earlier in my husband's career as a software developer, this situation felt very different. With two preschoolers at home, my own career consisted of reading books to my kids, playing with blocks, and very occasional consulting jobs.

I wasn't sure how to navigate the financial, physical, and emotional territory of Dave's unemployment. How much should I shield the children from the worry and stress? How much of that anxiety could I absorb without impairing my own well-being? And how could I encourage my husband in a discouraging situation? Who would encourage me as I faced the day-to-day demands of juggling bills, needs, wants, and uncertainty?

The main difficulty with this experience was that there was no guidebook saying how long we would be in the tunnel. An unemployment period of two months was something we could easily manage with savings, scrimping, and deferring as many expenses as possible. But we had no guarantee of the length of the "adventure," so it was difficult to know how to ration our gear along the way. If the length of the period of unemployment was specific and measurable, it might even be easier to understand how to ask for help. The nebulous long-term nature of the journey was troublesome.

While my husband was busy taking classes, working on his résumé, revving up his network of contacts, and signing up for unemployment compensation, I tried to figure out how to be a supportive partner in the process and a mother who didn't snap too often at her children. I vacillated between depression, optimism, rationalization, panic, planning, tradeoffs, and penny-pinching—my emotions and reactions were all over the map.

The Visa bill and the registration renewal for both cars came in the mail on the same day. I felt depressed. I had already bought plane tickets to go see my brother's new baby, but this didn't seem like such a good time for a trip, even though I needed the break.

The next day's mail brought a refund check from the insurance company that I didn't even know was coming. What a great provision! I was encouraged for a moment, but I figured the insurance company made a mistake and I'd have to send the money back. I told my friends that we would be fine, since we didn't have an extravagant lifestyle, but I sighed at the cost of health insurance under COBRA. I had a routine doctor's appointment and worried about the referral to a specialist I was given. Could I schedule this before our regular insurance ran out? I got tired of the everyday decisions and tradeoffs. First I gave up going out for any restaurant meals, but I wanted to keep my health club membership. Maybe next month I'd have to give up both.

And I wondered about my mothering style in this tunnel experience. Certainly I wanted to shield the kids from negative influences, but it wouldn't hurt them to know why we were always packing a snack in the car and never driving through Wendy's, even for the 99-cent menu. I wanted to model for them my faith that God would provide for us, but on the days when I had doubts, I'd rather not approach theology with an inquisitive five-year-old.

My childhood provided a few markers and insights into dealing with my situation. What did my mother do during the "bust" periods of the aerospace industry in the 1970s when my father went through several periods of layoffs? Since my mom had successfully shielded me from any worry over finances, I couldn't remember any great mothering insights for this part of my path.

My childhood memories were happy but didn't involve lots of stuff—we played in the woods behind the house, wore clothes my mom sewed, ate tuna casseroles for dinner, and went camping for vacations. That kind of frugal lifestyle apparently adapted well to lean periods, as I don't remember too many adjustments when dad was unemployed. The only cutback I can remember was that music lessons went away. That was a luxury my mom decided to trim. But my older sister started a job in a fast-food restaurant, and she found a teacher who could give us both lessons at a family discount. Even the music cutback didn't affect me deeply. It wasn't until my adult years that I realized what a generous act it was by my sister to pay for music lessons for her tagalong younger sister.

Childhood memories of these periods were simply of the oddity of having my dad at home during the day, rather than off at his office. Worry wasn't part of my vocabulary, so I guess my mom shielded me from that aspect of financial troubles. Certainly as a mom I wanted my children to have this same carefree, childlike trust that they didn't have to worry about housing, bills, food, or clothing. This wasn't a problem in the first few months of my husband's layoff, but the ongoing nature of the unemployment frayed my patience.

Christmas with preschoolers didn't have to be extravagant, so I scoured the thrift stores for new-looking toys to wrap up under the tree. I also took our collection of Christmas books, wrapped them up, and set them in a basket by the fireplace. We opened a book each night to read at bedtime.

The kids didn't need to be aware of the fact that Christmas only cost twenty dollars.

The problem came when the unemployment period stretched from weeks into months. I could defer my own needs and focus energy on other family members for a time, but that effort wore thin after several months. It was hard to admit that I needed help and encouragement as much as my husband did, just in different areas.

As I increased my work schedule, I started to resent the fact that I was still doing all the work around the house, even though our roles had reversed, albeit temporarily. And well-meaning friends seemed to focus more on my husband's needs than the fact that I also was in a situation where I needed help.

Help appeared not by magic but as a result of me learning to articulate needs. I needed a date with my husband, even if that date consisted of a walk around the park while our daughter was at parents' day out. I needed help around the house to accommodate my increased work schedule. I needed help with the financial details in terms of sharing the stress, even though I was perfectly capable of balancing the checkbook or figuring out the bills all by myself. Most of all, I needed to be able to say that I had needs—that it wasn't all about meeting the needs of my husband and children during this period.

> When everything seems to be going against you, remember that the airplane takes off against the wind, not with it.
>
> —Henry Ford

The reality of the recession invaded my daily life, but I could choose each day not to judge my self-worth by the balance in my checkbook. I could choose to enjoy the blossoms of spring. I could choose to check out an interesting

the mommy diaries

book from the library and take time by myself to read the book. I could choose to reach out to a friend and ask for help. I could choose to be a real woman who didn't have an answer for every question, rather than pretending that I was above the stress. As difficult as it was, I could even choose to accept a financial gift from friends.

Some days, I made positive choices and found hope even in a situation that went on for many months. Other days, it was easier to choose negativity and fear. But even in the midst of my needs and doubts, I still had the ability to choose. I could choose not to be in a recession of spirit and soul, even as I questioned the adequacy of my provisions for the journey.

Mother Helping Mother
by Susan Hitts

My inbox flashed with a new email from Kristina, a missionary friend in Malawi, Africa. The newsletter read much like the ones in the months before. She once again wrote of the extreme poverty and harsh living conditions that the native Malawians endured. Though she had expressed these facts many times, they always seemed somehow distant and detached from me and my life in America.

This new email was the first newsletter that I had received from Malawi since giving birth for the first time six weeks before. In the course of her letter, Kristina had written about a mother carrying her newborn baby in the village. The mother had tied together strips of rags to clothe her child; it was all that she had.

I stopped reading and looked over at my baby girl asleep in a swing beside me, dressed in beautiful clothes. I thought about my desires for her to have every good thing in life. How I had dreams for her future. How I wanted to meet all of her needs, always.

Suddenly this was no letter of distant Malawi facts like the many newsletters before had been. This was the story of a mother, a woman like me, who was limited not by her heart but by her means. I realized that as mothers, we both tried to provide the same good things for our children. However, the reality was that in this moment, my baby was dressed well, and hers wore rags.

I had never before felt such empathy for someone whom I had never met. I grieved for another mother's hurting heart as her circumstances kept her bound from providing even clothing for her child. She was no longer a nameless, faceless woman; she could be me. This was not another poor African baby; it was a loved child, like mine.

In that moment I decided that I could not stand idly by and know that a fellow mother was hurting and that a baby was in need. I could do something about this! By the time my husband came home from work, I was in tears, holding a box of my daughter's newborn clothes addressed to Kristina in Malawi, pleading with him to ship it for me. He called me from the post office to say that sending the box would take too long to help this family, but I insisted.

Around six months after she wrote the newsletter, Kristina was surprised to receive this box of baby clothes and a letter. I explained to her my desire to provide for a mother and child so that one baby doesn't have to live in rags and one mother can feel content in adequately clothing her child.

the mommy diaries

Kristina was able to give clothing not just to one family in need, but to ten.

Today, somewhere in Malawi, there are babies safely covered from the sun in my daughter's hand-me-down clothing, and there are mothers more at peace because their children have the clothes that they need. All because when I gave birth, I no longer saw people in need as just a distant fact. They were now real moms, real babies, and I really had to help.

Mommy's Needs, Baby's Needs
by Shelly Radic

Fascinated, my six-month-old daughter and two preschool friends watched the monkeys swinging from branch to vine, racing and tumbling and chattering together in wild abandon through the exhibit. Warm and breezy, it was the perfect day for our first trip to the zoo. With little ones well-occupied by the monkeys' antics, I allowed my mind to swing through the future of the new life growing within me. In my mind I saw a dark-haired baby stacking blocks alongside his fair-haired big sister. Leaping forward through the years, I envisioned a fifth birthday party that included dinosaurs and fire trucks, braces to correct an overbite, and hours and hours of cheering as round orange balls swished through a net.

I was well on my way through the teen years when a familiar sensation seared across my belly. Our perfect first trip to the zoo tilted toward terrible, and my imaginary journey through a little boy's life came to a crashing halt as we headed to the bathroom. Another miscarriage. The experience wasn't new, but handling the loss of one child in the midst of celebrating another's first trip to the zoo was. Before I became a mother, a miscarriage meant rolling into the fetal position and burrowing deep into a pile of comforters and pillows, filling tear-stained pages with angry rants and deep disappointment, and withdrawing into a world of solitude until the grief became bearable. Now I was at the zoo with three small children. Rolling into the fetal position wasn't an option. Neither was staying in the zoo bathroom.

Taking a deep breath, I prayed for courage and strength as we stepped back into the sunshine and moved toward the monkeys. I would be Wonder Mom, managing zoo fun in the midst of my crisis. Baby's needs, mommy's needs—I teetered back and forth between the two as we walked. One minute I

the mommy diaries

was the cheery adult sharing a silly song about monkeys jumping on a bed; the next I was gulping back tears that threatened to turn into a torrent of grief. Visions of Wonder Mom faded.

> For I am convinced that neither death nor life, neither angels nor demons, neither the present nor the future, nor any powers, neither height nor depth, nor anything else in all creation, will be able to separate us from the love of God that is in Christ Jesus our Lord.
>
> Romans 8:38–39

I settled onto a zoo bench to feed my baby and distribute animal crackers to our preschool friends while I waited for another sharp pain to pass. Mommy's needs, baby's needs. Stay calm. Admit you might need some help. Baby's needs, mommy's needs. Help with both. Wonder Mom was a myth.

Explaining my tears away as a tummy ache, I buckled up three car seats and headed for home. Drive safely. Don't frighten the children. Take deep breaths. Mommy's needs, baby's needs. Back home, I called for help, then emptied out a bucket of toys on the family room floor before curling up on the couch. Baby's needs, mommy's needs. I hung on to the knowledge that help was on the way.

Throughout the days that followed, a needy mom emerged, accepting offers for childcare and meals, appreciating the space help created for grieving. Time for grief allowed for healing. Healing brought strength to meet baby's needs. Mommy's needs, baby's needs. Accepting help meant meeting both.

A few weeks later, we were back at the zoo. Grieving wasn't over, but the silly monkeys made us smile.

Peanut Butter Love

by Elsa Kok Colopy

He was there every morning. I learned, after a few uncomfortable encounters, to turn my head at just the right moment to avoid eye contact. He looked so forlorn at the end of the exit ramp holding his cardboard sign, asking for help. It's not that I didn't care; I just didn't know what to do. I was a single mom with no money of my own, so how could I spare it for someone else? *Besides*, I thought to myself, *he could easily get a job. If I give him money, he'll probably just spend it on alcohol.*

My daughter felt differently. At only five years old, she wasn't so jaded. "Mama, what does that sign say?"

"It says he's out of work, and he needs help."

"Can we help him?" she asked, straining to watch him as we drove past.

"I don't think so, honey."

"But Mama," her eyes began to well up with tears. "Mama, he needs help! We can't just drive by."

I looked over at my girl. "I know, honey, and I love your heart. But we don't have any money to give him. We're barely making it ourselves."

"Yeah," she said, "but people have helped us, Mom. What about the lady that brought over groceries for us last week? We didn't even ask her for help and she did it anyway. Can't we share those?"

I thought for a minute. "Well, I suppose we could bring him a sandwich the next time we go past."

"Yes!" Sam exclaimed. "A sandwich! Peanut butter and jelly. That's my favorite; I'm sure it's his too. Everyone likes peanut butter and jelly."

I looked a little skeptical.

"They do," she insisted. "I promise."

The next day Sam helped me make a peanut butter and jelly sandwich. "Put extra peanut butter, Mom. Then it'll stick to the roof of his mouth. That's the best."

"Oh yes, that's important. Do you think we should get him something to drink too?"

"Absolutely!" she said. "And give him cheese puffs. Cheese puffs go good with peanut butter and jelly."

By the time we were done, we had the best lunch anyone under ten could hope for. I was nervous as we drove down the highway. What if he turned us down and it crushed Sami's heart? What if he was dangerous and reached in? Or even worse, what if he hated peanut butter and jelly?

We pulled off the exit, and I could feel my heart pounding. We came to a stop at the light and rolled down our window. The man came quickly over and looked surprised by the brown bag we handed him. "We don't have any money," I said, "so my daughter wanted to make you lunch." My eyes pleaded with him to be grateful, not to hurt her feelings, to say thank you.

> If you can't feed a hundred people, then feed just one.
>
> —Mother Teresa

I didn't have to plead. He bent over and looked in at Sam. "Thanks so much. That was very nice of you."

"It's peanut butter and jelly," she said proudly.

"I like peanut butter and jelly," he responded. Sam shot me a look: *See?*

"God bless you," he added.

Sam nodded and smiled. "You too."

As we drove away, I couldn't deny the warm feeling in my heart. Glancing over at Sam, I knew she was feeling the same way. "Good job, Sam," I said. "Way to show someone Jesus."

She patted my leg. "You too, Mama. You did good." I had to smile. I'd been wrong. And this time, for some odd reason, I didn't mind admitting it.

Dusty Trusty Guidebook
by Jami Kirkbride

"Okay," I called out, feeling frustrated inside. "Boys, let's meet on the couch." They all ran for the couch, and I headed for the kitchen. I'm sure they hoped I would reenter the room with snacks and a new attitude in hand. It had been a trying morning, and I was discouraged that my discipline wasn't bringing about changed hearts. I walked to the kitchen and found the Bible we'd used for devotions at breakfast that morning.

"Do you know what this is?" I asked as I sat sandwiched among their three little bodies.

"Yeah, it's the Bible," Jackson, the youngest, shouted without hesitation. Taylor, the oldest, hesitated. He knew there must be a catch to such an obvious question. And Carter sat watching intently, waiting and hoping that he could answer the next question a bit faster.

"You are right. It is the Bible. And what is the Bible?" I continued.

"A book," shouted the younger boys in unison.

"Yes," I agreed, "but it's a special book because . . ." I sat waiting for my oldest to come through.

the mommy diaries

"It is God's Word," Taylor answered with a little pride for helping me out.

"Yes, and God has given us special words here in this Bible. He gives us some rules, and he gives us some help. In fact, he even gives Mommy some directions in the Bible. Let me show you one." The boys watched with wonder, but I knew I'd better thumb quickly before my captive audience was lost.

"Right here." I used my finger to follow along in the Bible as I read. "'Discipline your son, and he will give you peace; he will bring delight to your soul' (Prov. 29:17). See, Mommy has been told by God to discipline you, and I have to obey God."

I sensed their little wheels turning. "Let's find another one." I flipped quickly to a verse I had heard my parents use many times. "Look: 'Children, obey your parents in everything, for this pleases the Lord' (Col. 3:20). And there he is talking to you. God gives me directions to discipline you, and he tells you to obey!"

I was shocked by their expressions. They sat motionless on the couch, still trying to take it all in. Then my oldest looked at me with a sly grin and said, "Does it really say that?" He smiled as if I were joking. I handed him the Bible and asked him to read both verses. He read them and still seemed captivated. The younger boys watched him and then asked him to show them where it was. There we all sat, crowded around one Bible, having a realization of the relevance of God's Word.

Our kids were being raised to do right. They were disciplined and taught manners. We attended church and did devotions each morning or at bedtime. They had learned how to pray and knew a lot about God. What I hadn't realized was that it carried an even greater meaning to them when they saw right there in black-and-white print in the Bible what God wanted from us.

A couple hours later my husband came home for lunch. The boys ran to the door. "Daddy, Daddy!" Jackson shouted.

"Wait till you see what we found in the Bible," Carter added.

"It really does say stuff about discipline, Dad," Taylor chimed in.

My husband looked at me questioningly. Little did he know the truths we had discovered together right there in the Bible. The boys took turns showing him the things we had read, straight from God's Word.

For our family, this was the beginning of using the Bible to help us do right. Since this was God's guidebook to us, we decided to really use it. Over the course of the next several months, the boys learned many verses that related specifically to discipline issues—speaking truth, self-control, sharing, loving, obeying, giving, and much more. The three boys learned over forty verses that year that could be useful in life and relationships. Their excitement about learning God's Word was contagious to me. Living by God's Word brought about a renewed sense of accountability for myself. The words in the Bible were put there for me to live by as well.

After that first day, I examined more closely my own attitudes about the Bible. I had been raised in a Christian home, had grown up attending church, and even read the Bible on my own each morning. But somehow, even with all that exposure, I had lost sight of the Bible being my guidebook for life's journey. In some ways it had become a special book with good stories of God's greatness and a lot of things that didn't necessarily apply to modern-day living. I remembered how I uttered some frustration about mothering and added, "Well, if they would just come with some sort of manual! I've never done this before. I don't know what to do!"

> For I am the LORD, your God, who takes hold of your right hand and says to you, Do not fear; I will help you.
>
> Isaiah 41:13

It had been easy for me to get caught up in the search for the best parenting and relationship resources. But I've been blessed by the number of times I've actually found a verse in the Bible that pertains to what I am struggling with or trying to teach my children. Sometimes I find myself overwhelmed by the job of teaching common courtesies, values, and character. Now when I am trying to teach these concepts and manners, I don't feel like I stand alone. After all, who is going to argue with God? God doesn't just leave me hanging. Whether I need answers, encouragement, or direction, I have a guide-book for the adventures ahead. It has been with me all along. I just need to pick it up and use it.

Helping Hands

by Celeste Palermo

"Go clean your rooms and then we'll go to the pool," I told my daughters on a sunny Saturday morning.

"Okay," they chirped in unison and, invigorated by the swimming proposition, dashed upstairs to tackle the chore.

Their enthusiasm soon melted like a Popsicle in the summer sun. Within minutes a deep wail boomed through the house from the room of my three-year-old. I found her sitting on her bed, face in hands, with alligator tears trailing down rosy cheeks. Her room, in typical toddler fashion, was littered with stuffed animals, clothes, dolls, and Happy Meal toys. The carpet was nowhere to be seen, hidden beneath the intimidating accumulation of stuff.

"I can't do it, Mama," Morgan cried when I peeked my head through the doorway. "It's too messy."

"Sure you can," I encouraged. "Just start with your dirty clothes and put them all in the hamper. Then put all your toys in the basket."

"I can't," she sobbed again, a soap opera star. "It's too messy. Can you help me?" she pleaded.

Then, like an echo, a second request followed the first. It was as if the walls had ears. "Can you help me too, Mom?"

My older daughter stood in the middle of her room, assessing the damage like a hurricane relief worker. She had waded into the wreckage with the best of intentions but became overwhelmed and was now just holding her ground, waiting for help to come.

"I need your help too, Mom. Can you please help me too?"

Her words triggered a poignant epiphany. Recently I'd gone back to work outside the home after being an at-home mom for several years. I thought my job, writing deadlines, and family commitments would be manageable, but I hadn't yet found a rhythm. Stacks of papers and piles of mail engulfed my home office, laundry seemed to have a secret source of Miracle-Gro, we had only one bathroom with toilet

the mommy diaries

paper, and I desperately needed to get my roots done. I felt overwhelmed, unable to catch up.

"If I could just get my feet on the ground," I told my husband a few days before, "I know I'd be fine."

"You need your mom" was all he'd said. I did need her, but I hadn't called. I didn't want to impose, but I also didn't want to admit I needed help. But I did. Just like my girls, I needed the reinforcement. Whether she actually helped me dig out of my disarray or just provided encouragement and direction, her presence would give me the reassurance to know that I'd be okay despite the chaos.

I helped my girls clean their rooms, and then we spent the afternoon at the pool. That night, after baths and bedtime stories, I tucked them into bed—and then I called my mom. "Mom, can you come for a few days?" I asked her. "I need your help."

"Sure," she said, and she booked her ticket.

At some point along my mothering journey, I came to the mistaken conclusion that if I had to ask for help, it was a sign of weakness, an indication I couldn't "cut the 'mom' mustard." It's so not true. The truth is, we all need help sometimes. God used my daughters' messy-room requests to remind me it is okay to ask for assistance when you need it. It takes a lot of courage to admit we need help—but then again, it takes a lot of pluck to even enter the ranks of motherhood, not to mention the shambles of a messy playroom.

Mothering is an adventure, an ongoing process of growing up, with a learning curve comparable to climbing Mount Everest. Realizing I do not have to be a one-woman mom-show was a big lesson in parenting and life. It gives me a

Ways to Accept Help

Trade babysitting with a friend so you can each run errands without kids.

Encourage your spouse to take on certain responsibilities with household chores, and then be happy, not critical, with the outcome.

Praise your children for pitching in with daily chores, such as morning and bedtime routines, mealtimes, and day-to-day responsibilities such as bed making and laundry.

Understand that extended family members can offer valuable advice and input. Accept their good intentions and let them help you when they offer.

Sign up to make meals for moms in need. Then accept the meals graciously when it's your turn to receive the meals.

Don't let resentment grow when you feel overburdened. Ask for help, clearly defining what it is you need and how much you appreciate support.

Reach out to a licensed counselor or trusted minister for mental, emotional, or spiritual support in times of need. There is no reason to be alone in your pain.

Talk honestly and openly with a women's prayer group, turning your deepest worries over to prayer.

Keep in mind that by asking for help, we can model this healthy behavior for our children. Not only will they be able to ask for assistance in their early years without shame or fear of judgment, but later, in the teen years, we may just save their lives. According to a 2007 report from the Centers for Disease Control, teen suicide rates are on the rise, and we need to encourage our children to reach out for help when they feel isolated, alone, and depressed. If we open ourselves up for physical, mental, spiritual, or emotional assistance in times of need, maybe our children will be more likely to do so as well.

the mommy diaries

humility I didn't know before I had children and along with it, a release from perfectionism. Recognizing my own limitations has made me a softer, more understanding parent. I know the messy-room overwhelmed feeling my daughters experienced that day. I get it, because sometimes the messes of my own life are just too big for me to handle too. So when I find myself flailing in the deep end, I look to my husband, my parents, and especially my God, "a very present help" (Ps. 46:1 KJV). And inevitably, like a lifeguard at the pool, helping hands lift me out of the water as soon as I begin to flounder.

Seeking Help . . . Every Day

Retraining ourselves to view asking for help as a necessary life skill can be hard. It might very well take several failed attempts before we finally summon up enough courage to actually do it. But once we do, we find the joys that arise from networks built on helping one another. We discover we aren't the only ones who need help. And we learn the value of bringing in a fresh perspective, new skills, and resources that differ from our own.

By giving and receiving help, we come full circle and realize the beauty of working together. Our gifts touch a greater number of lives instead of growing stagnant in our own families. Our own experiences grow richer and deeper because we've encountered something beyond ourselves with a beauty all its own. Practice the art of seeking out help. You might be surprised by what you find.

Utilizing Guidebooks and Gear

1. When was the last time you asked for help?
2. How hard is it for you to ask for help? What do you think holds you back?
3. Oftentimes failure to seek out aid from someone else stems from an issue of pride. What has got you thinking you are capable of handling it all on your own?
4. Do you view offers of help as debts you must pay off as quickly as possible?
5. What will it take for you to view the help you receive as acts of grace with no return favors expected?

5   Perspective

Embracing the View from the Summit

If you have ever been mountain climbing, you know that during the ascent, you don't get a lot of eye candy. In fact, you spend a lot of time staring right into the face of a rock—sometimes only a few inches away from your own face. Your muscles ache, your fingers dig into rough pockets of stone, and your toes almost cramp as they grip for dear life. But everybody knows this isn't why you do it. The reward comes at the top, once you hoist your body over the uppermost edge of the rock and stand up to take in the view from the summit.

From this angle, things look a lot different. In fact, they often look like a separate world altogether. Instead of focusing on a small area of red rock plastered two inches from your face, you take in miles and miles of undulating curves, peaks, and precipices—each a slightly unique hue. You notice the vegetation creeping on the Earth's floor, the clouds and birds sweeping across the sky. While climbing, you feel grounded, alert, part of every bit of action. The ascent is you—all about you. And suddenly, when you reach the summit, you're just a speck on the top of a rock in the midst of a most glorious display of beauty and purpose. Wow.

There is nothing quite like a change in perspective to turn your thinking around. The day-to-day act of mothering can feel an awful lot like climbing up a mountain wall. Our bodies ache, our spirits grow tired, and we often find ourselves face-to-face with a snot-nosed, weepy, whiny child. In moments like these, it can be hard to grasp the deeper meaning behind all we do. Finding fulfillment or peace can seem downright impossible. But when life allows for those brief but precious glimpses of what things might look like from the top, we gather strength and renewed purpose for our journeys as mothers. It's then that we realize we're working toward a goal and that the rewards from our summit couldn't be any sweeter.

Learning to Live with Plan A
by Ronica Stromberg

My son, Josiah, had just turned four years old when he was crippled in a car accident. He spent the next year and a half going through three surgeries, four body casts, and the accompanying recoveries. He remained bedridden a large part of the time, and when he was able to get around, it was often by dragging himself across the floor, his legs trailing behind him. After one surgery, Josiah was confined to bed for the usual six weeks but could not sit up and could only lie on his right side and his back.

What kind of life is this for a four-year-old? I found myself asking day after day. *Why did God allow this to happen to*

the mommy diaries

Josiah? I could see no good coming from any of it. And what made everything worse was that Josiah was so young and innocent that he didn't realize all that had been stolen from him. He just wanted to end his medical treatments now.

One day he was lying in our living room in an A-frame cast, and he said to me, "Mommy, we don't have to see the doctor again. It's okay if I never walk. I'll just lie in this same spot for the rest of my life." His words tore at my heart. *What could be God's purpose in this?* I kept trying to discern a plan B for Josiah's life. He was not yet in kindergarten but already the accident had eliminated sports opportunities and career options such as serving in the military. So where was God going with all of this?

Josiah entered kindergarten weak, fragile, and limping. While the other kids played during recess and physical education, Josiah sat restricted to the classroom, playing with Legos. He again took his limitations well, but my heart still broke for him.

"Isn't there anything else he can do during those times?" I asked his teacher.

"The only other thing we can offer then is music," she replied.

I enrolled Josiah in piano lessons. He excelled at piano; his teacher said he had a "natural ear" for music and was gifted. And Josiah loved performing, even playing solo at his kindergarten graduation.

Although I wasn't about to foist on Josiah the high expectation that he become a piano virtuoso, I could see the joy he was taking in piano. And slowly I began to see a change in my own attitude. While before I had been so frantically trying to discern a plan B for Josiah's life, now a new line of thoughts kept nudging at me: *What if Josiah is living plan A for his life? What if God always intended him to be crippled at age four? If this is plan A, why am I searching for plan B? Josiah might already be living the best plan for his life.*

He entered first grade with the same limp he had carried in kindergarten, but his teachers noted how happy he was. "He's always laughing and smiling," one said. "We can count on him to cheer others up. He's so happy, and he never gives up."

I drove up to school one day during recess and saw what she meant. Josiah was outside playing catch with some other boys. Sometimes they threw the ball to him, sometimes not, but he always went after it. He hobbled behind the other boys, unable to keep up. He tried to wrest the ball away from one boy—unsuccessfully. He stood in the line of the toss to have a better chance of catching the ball. No go. He continued playing, his every move seeming to say, "Look what I can do." I sat in my car and did just that. Josiah bounded before me, a firecracker of a handicapped boy—laughing, jumping, shouting, and living life in all its fullness . . . his life, as unmistakably laid out in plan A.

All along I had felt certain Josiah's accident was a wrong turn in his life. I couldn't see beyond all the negatives I thought would surely overshadow any chance at a fulfilled life. And yet now I am beginning to see the positives it has brought about. Josiah doesn't look at life and see what he can't do; he sees what he can do. Perhaps it wasn't a wrong turn after all.

Puff

by Diane Jasper

One hot afternoon I was lying flat on the couch, exhausted, while my two-year-old, Annie, ran circles around me. She was playing and jabbering and being a typical sweet, fun-loving, active toddler. Just watching her made me tired! I looked over and said to her, "I wish you could give Mommy some of your energy." She smiled at me, ran over, and with great big cheeks blew a big puff of air into my mouth.

We giggled, but it didn't work. I was still flat-out tired. But something sparked in me: *This reminds me of something— what is it?* Then I remembered the creation story, when God made Adam alive by breathing a puff of life into his nostrils. I was startled by how profound my little girl's instincts had been. This physical flatness seemed somehow connected to the dull, hollow feeling in my spirit.

Annie's worried little face was pressed close to mine. "Are you okay, Mommy?" Her loving little face moved me almost to tears. Tired or not, my heart was thankful for this beautiful bundle of joy God had given me.

Suddenly I realized how much I had to be thankful for. The simple, good, everyday things I forgot so quickly. I breathed a prayer of thanks for my healthy, energetic child . . . and my health . . . and my family . . . and my home and car and good food . . . and . . . and. . . . The list snowballed as thankfulness poured out of me until I realized I was grateful for God's gift of life and breath itself. It was incredible how much vitality and vigor those thankful thoughts gave me in such a short time. The longer my thankful list became, the more my energy increased. I was revived and riding high, lifted up on a fresh breeze of faith.

the mommy diaries

Little Annie didn't know any of this when she tried to puff her energy into me, but that loving little puff helped me begin the process of reshaping and recharging my perspective. Maybe it *did* work after all!

Cocoa Box Sinks
by Jeanne Zornes

Even a doll family needs a home, and so as my daughter's doll play morphed from pretend-bottle-babies into mommy-and-daddy dolls, a bookcase came home from a yard sale to serve as their new abode. Sure, whenever we went shopping and she persuaded me to "just look" in the toy department, I hoped the custodian would quickly mop up the drool she left in front of the doll accessories shelves. Plastic kitchens! Plastic dressing chambers! Plastic pools and cabanas! Plastic family rooms! All, of course, for a price.

Grandma indulged her Mr. and Mrs. Doll with a hot pink Corvette and a paler pink camping van. But Mom and Dad weren't as generous with store-bought items. "I've got some fabric scraps," I told her. "We can cut some for blankets. We can turn over these old shoe boxes and make their beds."

A plastic tartar sauce cup from the fish and chips restaurant became the sink for the hole in a cocoa-box-turned-bathroom-vanity. Two small boxes made some semblance of a toilet, and a bigger one served as a tub. Mug gift boxes became the washer and dryer. And so on it went—the improvising of furnishings for her growing doll family in their three-story bookcase "house."

At her birthday, instead of buying doll outfits, I bought a pattern and sewed from scraps a whole wardrobe of tiny doll clothes. After the initial pout that we were "too poor" to buy nice toys from the store, she warmed up to what she was getting.

One day a friend who came over to play dolls was fascinated by the array of clothes and accessories in my daughter's play corner. They were altogether different from what she'd seen on the toy shelves. "And my mommy sewed this wedding dress with real scraps from somebody's wedding dress," my daughter bragged as she happily hopped her satin-and-tulle-garbed doll around the bookcase house.

I smiled. By making do, we didn't have to mortgage *our* house to outfit *her* playhouse. I also realized I was passing on a heritage of thrift. My parents had modeled for me the value of going without or creatively using what you have. My mother, an asthmatic, couldn't work, so we lived on Dad's wages from a cardboard box mill. Lessons they absorbed from growing up in the dark shadow of the Depression helped them live without everything the world offered. They learned the biblical value of contentment.

> That energy which makes a child hard to manage is the energy which afterwards makes him a manager of life.
> —Henry Ward Beecher

As I noticed how much abundance and waste characterized my children's world, I realized that modeling a simpler lifestyle would offer a needed check for an emerging "more and more" value system. I needed its discipline as well. Making dollhouse accessories with items I already had around the house reminded me to be content with what I had in my real world too.

the mommy diaries

Perspective from a Puddle

by Jami Kirkbride

"There you go," I mumbled as I handed my daughter her book. She carefully laid it on her lap with her doll, blanket, sippy cup, necklace, and numerous other items I'd just handed to her upon request. I had started the morning with patience, but now I seemed to be struggling to find the last ounce of it. We had just sent the oldest one off to school on the bus. Now the three little ones were all buckled snugly in their car seats. I breathed a little sigh and climbed into the car.

"Music, music," my eighteen-month-old daughter commanded from her seat. I could tell even at this early age that Savannah had a mind of her own, and she wasn't afraid to share it. The little boys shouted their requests from the far backseat.

"VeggieTales," Jackson shrieked with excitement.

"No, let's have Rubber Ducky," Carter exclaimed. On any other day, he would request VeggieTales. Why, I wondered, couldn't they just agree?

"Rubber Ducky, Rubber Ducky!" Savannah's vote tipped the scale.

Okay, I thought, *this morning the majority vote wins.* I reached for the CD with the bath songs and started the music. The music was upbeat and happy. The children sang along with the words. "Splish, splash, I was taking a bath . . . "

As we bounced down the long dirt road, my thoughts began to drift. The bath songs resonated throughout the vehicle, and I suddenly had an image of me as a mother. I was dressed in a big, floppy T-shirt. My hair was pulled back in a ponytail, and little tufts of hair fell on the sides. My makeup was smudged, and I looked a bit bedraggled. I knelt beside the bathtub in a puddle of water created from the splashes erupting from the tub. I sank a bit in the driver's seat. *Nothing about mothering is glamorous. I remember the days I worked and was regarded by my colleagues as a professional. I'm glad they don't see me now.* I slumped in my seat and thought of the other mothers out there. All of a sudden I felt lowly and pitiful. Other moms would be heading to work while dressed in their best and listening to their choice of adult music. I would head to preschool and just look plain and simple. No, I might just look as though I'd been through the wringer. My thoughts were on a downhill slope and headed nowhere but the slush pile. But I hadn't realized it just yet. I could feel my body melt into the seat, and a feeling of worthlessness passed over me like a fine mist.

The music continued to play this whole time. Before I knew it, we were on our second time through the songs. "Splish, splash, I was taking a bath. . . ." The volume hadn't changed. But all of a sudden I could clearly hear each of my children singing the songs. I looked in my rearview mirror and saw their smiles as they sang. They continued to sing without realizing I was watching them. They looked at each other and laughed as they sang rather loudly. Slowly, I began to see a picture of me as a mother. I saw myself giving the kids baths as we laughed and played. Their splashing and playing resulted in a puddle on the floor, but that didn't seem to matter too much. As I knelt next to the bath, I didn't think so much about my appearance, but I was happy. I was in the moment and enjoying the laughter and interaction. My spirit began to perk up a

What to Do with All Those Gifts?

Special shelf—Place your children's special creations on a designated shelf in the kitchen or living room for all to see. Your children will be proud of their contribution to the home decor, and the gifts will serve as a constant reminder that you are loved and appreciated.

Treasure box—Help each child create a treasure box by decorating an empty shoe box or plastic storage container. When they insist on keeping favorite sticks, rocks, feathers, or trinkets, help them store them safely in their own space.

Catch and release—When your children surprise you with a living worm, frog, or other critter, enjoy learning about this unique animal, and then gently return it to its family.

Vintage vase—Designate a quirky vase for the flowers your children bring to you. Keep it in your kitchen windowsill, and you'll never lack for fresh blooms.

bit. *I am affecting the lives of my four children*, I thought. *We have made this choice for our family and I am glad.* I don't do everything right, but we are a happy family and we love each other. I wouldn't change what I have when I am with them.

Then it dawned on me. In the course of this drive, no circumstance had changed. The children were still sitting in their car seats. No other person had spoken to me. The environment was still the same as it was just fifteen minutes before, silly bath songs still blaring. But what was the cause of my change of thoughts? How could I go from slumped in my seat feeling worthless to sitting happy and proud of my choices as a mother?

Slowly, I strung the thoughts of my ride together. I saw the course clearly. I was the one choosing my perspective. I could decide to see myself in either light. The events and circumstances of the ride remained unchanged. Only my perspective on my role as a mother, my children, and myself had changed.

I chose this journey. And while some portions of the adventure are challenging and discouraging, nothing could compare to the overall experience of mothering. Seeing their smiling faces, hearing their little giggles, and knowing I have an impact on their lives proves to be the most rewarding experience I could ever imagine. There may still be days I will muddle in my puddle, but my perspective can make the difference. When I get to the top of this summit, I want to look back and see the memories we have made along the way. And I *will* have a choice in my perspective.

Freefalling
by Tally Flint

Do you ever have that nightmare where you're falling through the air? At first it feels sort of fun, but then your body twists and turns as you try to reach for anything to hold on to before plummeting, presumably, to your death. Before experiencing impact, you bolt awake, gasping for air, wondering how something that started out so beautiful could take such a horrifying turn.

For me, that dream hits way too close to home with my mothering experience. On any given day, I go from feeling like I've got it all together—well-behaved children, successful potty training, a shower *and* mascara—to the brink of despair as I watch it all fall apart—a tearful tantrum, poopy underwear, and peanut butter smeared on my shirt. My heart sinks at the realization that I've lost all control, and I cringe at the thought of what that says about me as a mother. Who am I if I can't get my own family in order?

I came face to face with this struggle the summer before my daughter was born. I attended a picnic with friends at a large park not far from our home. My husband had to work that day, so I arrived solo, toting my then two-year-old son Thomas, my increasingly rotund belly, and the pasta salad for the potluck. During the course of the afternoon, I lost track of Thomas. One minute he'd been climbing the swing set; the next he'd disappeared.

I struggled up from my perch on the bench and calmly waddled around the playground, peeking into tunnels and around slides to see if he was simply hidden from my view. When that search turned up empty, I noticed a set of concrete stairs to the left of the playground and realized he'd probably headed down those, given his affinity for stairs of all kinds. My heartbeat picked up a bit, and when I peered over the top step and didn't see him, I told myself to calm down, that everything would be okay, he was bound to turn up any minute. Just as I reached the base of the stairs and headed out along the sidewalk, I noticed a woman leading a child by the hand, right in my direction. I squinted into the sun and realized, with a jolt of relief, that the hand belonged to Thomas.

We met in the middle of the sidewalk and I knelt down, looked Thomas dead in the face, and told him he was never to leave my side again. The woman gave me the once-over, taking in my burgeoning belly, and tsked, "He was down playing by the river." I could hear the unsaid implication in her tone. *Irresponsible mother. What business does she have getting pregnant again if she can't even keep her son from drowning?* Heat rushed to my face as I thanked her for returning my son. She gave me one last withering gaze before walking away.

My calm veneer suddenly cracked, and I pulled Thomas into a fierce hug. Tears sprang to my eyes and my insides felt like they would burst with all the "What ifs?" *What if he'd drowned? What if I'd lost him? What if the woman is right? What if I shouldn't be a mother?* The overwhelming fear that rushed through me brought me to my knees. I realized I'd never be able to fully protect my kids and in fact, I'd probably face even scarier episodes as they grew older. How in the world would I ever make it to their eighteenth birthdays?

We live in a frightening world, and as mothers, I think we're especially sensitive to the potential dangers we face. We even pride ourselves on our ability to protect our loved ones from them. When I lost Thomas, I certainly freaked out about what could have happened to him. But I also hated knowing that the woman who found him thought I was a bad mother, a failure. Doesn't it seem like there's something wrong with that picture? Shouldn't all of my energy have gone to concern for my son? What kind of mother lets pride rival her care for her babies?

I left the park that day with a bitterness in both my mouth and my heart. I was confused at my reaction as much as I was scared of what could have happened. And then, only a couple days later, I realized it wasn't about me. Yes, I had a responsibility to care lovingly for my kids, but their true security does not lie with me. I can't keep watch over them all the time, and really, it wouldn't be healthy for them if I did. I am not the one who gets to write the plan for their lives—God is. And he remains the only one fully equipped to do so. Ultimately, only he can protect them, and only he can lead them to the life for which he created them.

As a mom, I crave control but rarely have it. And there is something freeing in the knowledge that control really isn't my job to begin with—in being able to trust in someone else to take care of me and my own. Frankly, we all know God is much better at handling all of that than we ever could be. What have I been missing because I was too afraid to let go? What if the next time I find myself plummeting through the air, I remember to throw my arms out, let go of control, and see what happens when I let God keep me afloat? Perhaps I'll find that I'm not so much falling as flying. Maybe, just maybe, it isn't supposed to be a nightmare after all.

God's-Eye View
by Cheryl L. Steplight

Finally! After seven years, the house that we lived in was becoming *our* house. It no longer whispered Miss Clara's name, the sweet old lady from whom we had bought it. We pulled up green carpet and restored the hardwood floors. We freed the walls from the weeping willows that had been their previous identity. They gladly received crown molding and bold colors. We took down drapes that tied the green carpet and the weeping willows together like a holiday bow.

Sheers that allowed the sun to pour in replaced them. Yes, our house was now our home.

Despite feeling pleased, I saw one thing left to do. We had to get rid of the 1980s-style secondhand sofa and ottoman that now stuck out like a sore thumb. Just the thought excited me. My children didn't share the same sentiment, however. They were devastated. They whined and questioned the decision as if they had a vested interest in what was taking place. At first I thought they were just being children. They had never shown allegiance to our living room furniture—let alone the will to fight for it. But they were serious. They sat on the sofa with the principled determination of political protestors. And they refused to move. That is, until I informed them that they would be carried out with it and they too would travel to the home of bulk trash.

With heads and shoulders hung low, they slowly rose and dragged their feet as they meandered to the front porch. There they sat and watched as the furniture was placed outside for pickup. Then the tears began to flow. They watched. And they cried. And they sat. I was both surprised and tickled by their reaction. I stood inside and laughed the type of laughter that melts worries away.

As they took in their final glimpses of the old sofa, we were busy bringing up a leather sofa from the basement. It replaced the drapes by serving as the bow that would tie together the bold colors, hardwood floors, and brilliant sunlight. The piano and television found new arrangements as well. The room felt completely new, and I was beyond satisfied.

When the children came inside, they quickly replaced their tears with wide eyes, open-mouthed grins, and cheers

the mommy diaries

of excitement. They turned around in the middle of the room to take in the changes from every point of view.

"Wow! Look at our new house!" they screamed. "We love it, Mom!" They forgot the old furniture in an instant. They ran to sit on the "new" sofa in the "new" room, and they beamed with delight. They praised our hard work and the decisions we'd made. I basked in their approval and took pleasure in knowing that they welcomed our "new" home.

> I consider that our present sufferings are not worth comparing with the glory that will be revealed in us.
> Romans 8:18

As any good mother would do, I shared with them the significance of getting rid of the old to make room for the new. And they got it. But so did I as God began to speak to me. He reminded me that like my children, I pout and cry over things that once served a purpose but are now worn and need to be replaced. In his wisdom, he decides when those things must go, but I protest and am hurt by the thought. All the while, he has plans of replacing what I'm holding onto with something better, that's better for me, and that would bring me wide-eyed delight. He knows exactly what he has in store for me. And he knows that it would far exceed any of my expectations.

A Mixture of Colors
by Kari J. Glemaker

By the time he was three, we knew that Josh was "different." He just seemed to view his world through a different set of lenses than other kids. As his mom, all I knew was that he struggled in social settings—especially in preschool.

Nearly every day, as other moms stood in line to pick up their child from preschool, I was greeted by "Mrs. Glemaker, the teacher needs to speak with you." As the other mothers looked on, I stepped to the side so that I could hear about Josh's day. "Today he wouldn't answer to Josh. He said he was Batman," or "Today he was Robin Hood and everyone in class were the bad guys. He tried to 'round them up' to take them to Nottingham, including the teachers." I began to dread the end of the school day and the parent-teacher meeting. Later I realized that I stood alone as the other mothers grouped together to plan playdates and after school fun. Josh and I were not included—I was "Josh's mom" and he was the infamous "Josh."

One day while waiting for the school day to end, I noticed the hall lined with the most recent artwork from the class. The teachers had taken pieces of plain, textured wallpaper and cut them into the shape of a vase. Out of the vases the children had finger painted flowers of all sizes and colors. I was very impressed with the variety of flowers represented in these preschool masterpieces. As I looked at all the paintings, I came upon one that really caught my eye and eventually made me smile. This painting did not look like the others. Instead of flowers upright in the vase, this child had the flowers cascading over the vase. Not only were there flowers, but this child's contribution stood out with greenery not seen in the other wall displays. The viewer had to really look at this piece to see the beauty of the individual flowers as they were swirled together to form a beautiful mix of colors. My smile turned to a look of pride as I recognized the name of this artist—the infamous Josh.

> ## Just Be You!
>
> Like Josh, mothers don't always fit a certain mold. Some mothers are gifted chefs, while others can barely manage to make toast without the fire alarm sounding. Some can whip up a homemade costume in hours, while others struggle to select the right size from the store shelves.
>
> Don't try to force yourself into an image that you have of mothers. You'll quickly lose perspective and feel like a failure. Instead, focus on the things that make you happy and the talents you can offer. It may not look to the rest of the world like you're doing a great job, like the teacher's view of Josh compared to his peers, but the people who really matter will appreciate you for being yourself. After all, it's you they love.
>
> —Julie Cantrell

That day was a true turning point in my awareness of being Josh's mom. He is different than the "typical" child, but I learned to celebrate and honor his uniqueness. Today that "cascading flower" painting hangs framed in our family room, and Josh continues to bring a mixture of beautiful colors to our life.

Transition Pains
by Carol Kuykendall

One Saturday afternoon shortly after our youngest child left home for college, my husband Lynn and I wandered into a gourmet kitchen store in our downtown mall. I'm not sure why, since we're not gourmet cooks. Soon we joined a small group watching a woman make pasta.

Gracefully and easily, she kneaded the floury dough, fed it into one side of the pasta maker, and voila! Out came long, perfect pieces of pasta. Like magic. Like simplicity.

She then passed out portions of fresh-cooked pasta for us all to taste. Lynn and I looked at each other, suddenly smitten with the same idea. In this new season of life, we could reinvent ourselves and become pasta-makers. Instantly I pictured how we would invite people over for dinner; they would sit around our kitchen counter, watching us make pasta, and then rave about it later at the dinner table. They'd probably even tell their friends about our now-famous pasta dinners.

"Let's get one," I semi-begged. Lynn agreed, and so we did, spending more than we should have on a whim.

Later that night, amid a flour-spattered kitchen with long, ugly pieces of pasta hanging from everywhere to dry, we both ran out of patience and had a big argument. "This isn't as much fun as I thought it would be, and I hate sticky messes that I have to clean up," I muttered.

"That *we* have to clean up," Lynn shot back, putting pieces of the pasta maker in the sink.

At that moment I decided I didn't like pasta, I didn't like this silly machine, and I wasn't even sure I liked Lynn just then.

We got beyond that evening, and soon I put the whole thing in better perspective. I could see that we were merely trying to navigate our way through one of the many transitions in our family and our marriage. We'd been in this messy place before. After I weaned each of our three children, Lynn and I planned an overnight to celebrate our new freedom, and I remember struggling with missing the baby more than enjoying the freedom.

When our kids were growing up and at home less often, we decided to find a new activity for just the two of us. So we signed up for six sessions of country western dance lessons at a nearby cowboy restaurant. After the first lesson, I realized that dancing together can bring out either the best or the worst in your marriage. Some couples glide effortlessly around the floor in perfect step with each other, surely symbolizing the harmony of their relationship. Others, like us, move more clumsily, stepping on each other's feet and quibbling about who's leading and who's following.

But I remember something else about those lessons. By the sixth one, we had learned to laugh at our efforts instead of blame each other, and we'd actually gotten better at dancing together.

The pasta-making fiasco was similar. By the time we agreed to donate the nearly-new machine to a fundraiser at our church, I kind of hated to see it go. Boxed up on a shelf in our garage, it had been a visual reminder that the journey of our marriage faced some bumps in the transitions. But bumbling our

> In the middle of every difficulty lies opportunity.
> —Albert Einstein

way through those places makes us stronger and better prepared for the road ahead.

Discipline 401 Honors
by Shelly Radic

"Your children are so well-behaved. How do you do it?"

"You just choose an approach to discipline and stick with it," I'd reply. But in my mind I would add, "It is really not all that difficult. If you stick with the program, children will respond."

And I really thought that was true, until one day something happened that changed my perspective: baby number four stopped taking naps and started exploring the world—on his own terms.

Dressers became stairsteps and a platform for crib diving. Windows became escape routes to the backyard. Plastic patio chairs became mechanisms to launch an assault on the backyard gate. Closed doors were for opening and closing; locked doors were for breaking and entering. Items on high shelves inspired climbing expeditions.

Time-out meant time to figure out a new way of using ketchup. Taking away toys meant taking apart the stroller. Of course, the stroller wasn't really missed, because who needs a stroller when your own two legs take you places with lightning speed? Places your mother finds dangerous—like the six-foot-deep construction pit on a street two blocks away.

Consequences were forgotten in five minutes; happy face stickers looked better on cats than on behavior charts. Missing fun outings left more time to figure out how to get on the roof.

> If you obey all the rules, you miss all the fun.
> —Katharine Hepburn

Discipline wasn't so easy with a turbo-charged, alarmingly curious, and unfazed-by-consequences child. Consistent discipline meant trying a new approach each day. Other moms began dropping discipline hints, suggesting I be more consistent. "Just choose an approach to discipline and stick with it," they'd say.

the mommy diaries

"What a great idea," I'd reply. In my mind I'd add, "If you only knew." I was humbled.

Constant vigilance and redirection became my vanguard methods. I couldn't wait for preschool to start so I'd get a break from the constant battle. I smiled with understanding at moms in the grocery store chasing toddlers down the aisle. I felt their pain.

I learned a consistent approach to discipline meant more than three tries. Or thirty. Sometimes it took three hundred. Eventually my turbo toddler began to understand consequences and even remember them more often. Mad Science classes provided an outlet for chemical curiosity. Whizzing down a hill on a skateboard replaced the thrill of climbing on the roof. A helmet was included most of the time. We're still working on that one.

The Day I Took Flight
by Mary Beth Lagerborg

When my friend Mimi and her husband moved to Quito, Ecuador, as missionaries, I was ecstatic when the opportunity came to visit them. The only problem was the flight to get there. Denver to Miami. Miami to Quito. This would be hard for a mom who hated to fly.

As usual, the takeoffs and landings were the worst. Isn't that when planes usually crash? I closed my eyes, held my cupped right palm cradled in my left in my "praying position," and lifted this mantra: *Lord, please keep us safe. Please keep us safe.* What would happen to my boys if I went down in the plane? Logically thinking through options for my three sons' care didn't help. I inevitably came to the same conclusion: they couldn't possibly make it without me.

Despite my fears, I arrived safely. Mimi acquainted me with their home, the marketplace, their friends. Then Mimi was to speak at Shell Mera, a mission station on the edge of the jungle, and I was to accompany her.

We took a taxi to the airport in Quito, then walked to a hangar housing a little three-passenger Mission Aviation Fellowship airplane that looked like a toy my boys would play with . . . and crash into the dirt. The missionary pilot's job was to take missionaries and supplies for them to their homes in remote areas. To be most efficient, the pilots combined trips when possible. And so it was that Mimi and I found ourselves sharing the plane with career missionary Rachel Saint.

Rachel, I knew, was someone just below Mother Teresa when it came to amazing Christian women. Her brother, Nate Saint, was the missionary pilot who had been martyred with Jim Elliot and three other men on a sandbar in the Ecuadorian jungle. Soon afterward, Rachel had gone to live with the tribe who had murdered him, and she had spent the rest of her life ministering to them. There she sat, looking like someone's grandma. She was white-haired and fair, elderly, and ill with cancer. She had come to Quito to see a doctor and was returning to her home in the jungle.

We took Rachel home first. We skirted peaks in the Andes from our tiny seats, then dropped through clouds over jungle treetops so tightly packed they looked like bunches of broccoli. As we approached the mud airstrip, a brown swath in the trees, our pilot circled over the sandbar in a wide, looping, brown river where the men had been martyred about thirty years before.

We circled the airstrip once for an inspection. The pilot said it was wetter than he expected, but he'd give it a try. He landed perfectly, but the tires pulled through sticky mud. "I'm not sure we can get back out of here today," he said. Rachel graciously invited us to stay the night with her in the jungle. I told Mimi that I didn't camp and was quite sure I didn't have whatever shots were needed here and that we really needed to go home.

Meanwhile the Huaorani Indians, anticipating Rachel's homecoming, appeared from the jungle and swarmed around the plane to greet her. Mimi pointed out to me an elderly woman named Dayuma who had made contact with the missionaries on the sandbar. She was now a Christian, a leader in her people group.

Rachel and the pilot disembarked, but Mimi and I stayed high and dry in the plane as the pilot and some of the men picked up the tail of the plane and wheeled it around so that we faced the way we had come up the airstrip.

The pilot said he would at least give it a try and invited me to sit next to him up front. I peered at all the round dials as we bounced up the strip, gathering speed. "How are your stomachs?" he asked. "Fine," we answered. So near the end of the airstrip he launched us straight up! Clearing the trees, he turned in a semicircle and came back over the airstrip, flapping the wings in fun just over the heads of the Indians. Then at the end of the strip we shot straight up again.

Well! In my entire life up to then and since, I have rarely been so excited. And I kept thinking, "If my boys could only see me now! They wouldn't believe what Mom is doing today!" A strong maternal instinct had kept me hunkered down as if among the jungle trees. It had made of me a keep-safe mom.

A cautious mom. A carefully planning mom. All good, but I realized that I also wanted my sons to see me—and I wanted to see myself—as a mom, a woman, who also grabbed the adventure of life and took a risk now and then. I had liked life responsibly salted, but realized I also like a good shake of pepper—and a jalapeño now and then!

I've traveled farther in life and more freely since that day I took flight. I have to think that my sons have too.

Olivia's Grace
by Susan Besze Wallace

I can actually smile now when I see the box. For years I would touch it, round and satin under my bedside table, and feel vomit in my throat and an aching in my chest. Pictures of her are in there, as well as the hospital blanket that still bears blood from her precious 11.8-ounce body. But she has become far more than a stack of mementos and dead flowers.

Such perspective was hard-earned and heaven-sent. After three years of trying to become a mom and a sixteenth-week miscarriage in our Ford Explorer, dozens of injections and thousands of dollars resulted in her new life. We had some weeks without worry. And then tests. And then bed rest. And then hospitalization. And then the unthinkable: news that our daughter was basically starving to death inside the womb and too small to survive outside of it. She was born at twenty-six weeks, weighing less than a can of Coke—the most beautiful thing I'd ever seen, even though she died during labor. She spent the night nestled between her parents

the mommy diaries

in a hospital bed, a ring I still wear slipped all the way up to her shoulder. When the sun started to come up, somehow I handed my dead daughter to a nurse, knowing I'd never see her again in this life. Little did I know this was not the end of Olivia Grace.

Postpartum, without a baby to smell. Milk coming in, no one to feed. Back to work, as a journalist, covering the fallout from the Columbine massacre took on new meaning. How *dare* I think I understood what those families felt. There were lunches in the cemetery. Baby showers I couldn't stomach. And a grief group where I started to hope for a new normal to settle in.

Many nights I stared up at my ceiling fan so long and hard I thought it would fall on me. And sometimes I hoped it would. I screamed at God on occasion, but I also learned to lean on him and go to him with my anger and my yearning. I couldn't wait for some lightning bolt fix to make the hurt go away. God didn't take my baby. But he did take away any idea that I was in control.

We continued to try to become parents, miraculously hopeful again and yet understandably terrified. We considered adoption, and through the physical required by the process, I found out I had thyroid cancer. Once it was removed, we tried again. We refinanced the house for one try at in vitro fertilization and were blessed with a son, born perfect with the help of blood thinners and a great doctor.

Even as a new mom, the pain of losing a child was still like a burden I carried daily. If I wore it well, it made me stand taller and stronger. I might even forget it was there for a few hours. But if I were to hunch over, to give in, I knew it could bend me permanently into bitterness.

I signed up for an anonymous prayer partner program in my MOPS group. Anxious to learn about my secret pal, I scanned her information form and lost my breath. She too had a daughter born in 2000. On the same day. At the same hospital. But hers, of course, left the building in her mom's arms.

I wasn't sure I could stomach the cruelty of gifting and encouraging a mom who would always remind me of what I'd lost. But I did. Moreover, I grew to love her entire family. That next year they asked us to celebrate her daughter's birthday. I still considered Olivia's day sacred, spending it solo and graveside. But on that May 3, I also ventured to Chuck E. Cheese's, marveling at the transformation rolling out in my life.

Thanks to my lifeless baby, I am a different kind of mother. Poop does not make me nauseous. Finding a baby's snot on my boob or throw-up in a crib—it's nasty, but it's a privilege. When I hear "Mommy" forty-seven times in sixty seconds, I somehow can take a deep breath and answer patiently. When my husband leaves on a last-minute work trip and a date with a friend goes up in smoke, I can have a sing-along at bedtime instead of a pity party. That's all because of her.

I'm far from a perfect mom. We all get angry and tired and fed up with endless floor sludge, laundry mountains, and bickering siblings. I've been known to eat double-digit Oreos at 10:00 p.m. as solace when my husband travels for a week.

But truly, I can see each day with Zach—and his miracle brothers Luke and A.J.—as gifts straight from God. Yes, now there are three. Somehow I have become *that* woman, the

> ## How to Heal after a Miscarriage
>
> **Do not blame yourself for the loss.** Miscarriages occur naturally and usually cannot be prevented.
>
> **Accept that there may not be an answer.** Despite many medical advances, parents are not always given a reason why they lost their baby.
>
> **Honor your child.** Whether in private, with close family members, or with friends, it is important for you to memorialize your child.
>
> **Work through your grief.** Not only are you dealing with the extraordinary pain of losing a child, you are also hormonally unbalanced. Allow yourself time to rest, grieve, and face the wide range of emotions that will surface.
>
> **Share the pain.** Accept that your husband has also lost a child, and talk openly with each other about the experience.
>
> **Have hope.** Just because you've had one miscarriage doesn't mean you won't be a mother in the future.

one that raises eyebrows when she walks through the store as you say, "You have your hands full, don't you?"

I still see little girls in pink tutus at McDonald's and sometimes still can't believe that I will never braid my daughter's hair or buy her wedding dress or see her become a mom. But who knew I'd be more excited than my boys to take them to the NASCAR Café on vacation? I relish building space shuttles out of cardboard and pirate ship birthday cakes. I'm actually saving tin cans so they can water gun them off our backyard wall. Their enthusiasm, noises, and ebullient zest for life—what a delight it is for someone who had only sisters to discover her inner five-year-old boy.

When I was trying to become a parent, I wanted so much to hear God speak plainly to me. These days I realize he was—through the desires of my heart. There's no other way to explain why my quest for a biological child never wavered, how I survived living barren in a child-infested suburb, how I continued to work, and how my faith increased. I think he was preparing me for the perspective necessary to parent three amazing little boys.

I have many questions to ask God one day. But for now, six big blue eyes tell me all I need to know. I give them my best, ever mindful of the fact I never got the chance to give her anything.

Her things are in the box. But she is, and forever will be, inside of me.

Keeping Perspective . . . Every Day

When we're immersed in the preschool years, it can be hard to take a step back and bask in the long-term benefits our hard work promises to reap. As we wipe baby bottoms, kiss boo-boos, and explain why the sky is blue for the one hundredth time, we're most likely thinking about what's in the freezer that can pass for a semi-nutritional supper—not about the responsible young women and men we're raising to impact the world for the better.

But setting aside time to gain a new perspective inevitably energizes our efforts and gives us the pat on the back we need to carry on. Such encouragement might come in the form of a heart-to-heart with another mom, a chance to let Dad take care of the kids so we can sit back and watch the fun, or one-on-one time with our children, when we can really take in the little persons they're becoming.

Nobody ever said this journey would be easy, but we can all attest to how much better the descent is once we've caught a glimpse from the summit. In fact, it usually makes us want to begin the ascent all over again. That's some view!

Embracing the View from the Summit

1. At what times do you feel you could especially use a dose of perspective in your mothering journey?
2. How do you get those doses?
3. Are there practical ways you can schedule little "views from the summit" in your life to help you maintain a sense of purpose and power in the work you do as a mom?
4. When was the last time someone noticed the hard work you do and commented on it?
5. Can you learn to trust that God—in all his compassion, wisdom, and power—sees a bigger picture than you do and will faithfully bring you to a place of purpose of which you never dreamed?

6   Hope

Expanding My Limit

In the midst of any pursuit, inevitably a sliver of doubt arrives, creeping into your thoughts and leaving you wondering how you're going to make it. The triathlete wonders if she has enough energy left inside to make it through the last leg. The backpacker looks ahead to a mountain of steep switchbacks and gulps to find the breath to keep climbing. The white-water rafter plunges beneath a rapid and struggles to resurface.

The adventure of mothering is fraught with times when doubt creeps in and we wonder if we really have what it takes to finish the job. When the pain of labor intensifies beyond our imagination, we ask, "Will this baby ever make it into the world?" After months of navigating the adoption process, when delay after delay seems to thwart our plans, we doubt if the child of our dreams will actually be ours after all. As children age and we find ourselves in the throes of power struggles, frightening illnesses, and the agony of learning to let go, our future can seem pretty bleak.

And then, as if on cue, hope arrives, and we dig in and find just what we needed to keep going. A friend cheers us on from the sidelines; a child grins and reminds us why we love them so much; God speaks to our heart and we discover we're not alone. Hope: our rescue in times of trouble, our companion on paths of loneliness. How would we ever survive without it?

Still Beautiful
by Christine Jeske

During our first two years as parents, my husband and I worked in China as English teachers. When our daughter Phoebe was just seven months old, my mother became seriously ill. We decided that my husband would stay in China to finish the semester's teaching responsibilities while Phoebe and I made the trip back to the United States to see family. It was on the way back to China that I spent some of the most nightmarish fifteen hours of my life.

Knowing that traveling alone with a seven-month-old baby across twelve time zones would be no easy journey, I planned the trip carefully. I would keep her awake until the plane left, then let her take a long nap while I ate my dinner and got some rest early in the trip. I would arrive in Beijing with just a few hours of layover time, then catch a plane to our home on the west side of China.

My first problem hit with the news that my flight was delayed. Two long airport hours later, we boarded. I tucked my overtired and irritable infant into a seatbelt on my lap, marveling at just how narrow they made airline seats. The man next to me explained politely that he badly needed sleep, then strapped on headphones and a face mask.

Another hour passed in delay. When the engines finally roared into motion, I knew I would miss my connecting flight. That meant finding accommodations alone in Beijing, China. Phoebe seemed as nervous as me, frantically nursing while I deflected her kicking legs from the man next to me. Already I had crossed and uncrossed my legs a dozen times, banging my ankles on the seat in front of me.

Whether it was the pressure changes bothering her ears, overtiredness, or the overwhelming unfamiliarity, she refused to fall asleep. When our long-overdue dinner arrived, Phoebe threw a fit. She threw her little head back and nearly wriggled out of my arms while I tried to lift her above the food tray clamping me into my seat. I squeezed my hips around the tray, hoping that standing up would ease her claustrophobic panic, but the food cart next to me trapped me. I stood there feeling the stares of the entire airplane for endless moments while the old man across the aisle debated over his chicken or beef choice. I ate next to nothing.

For the next eight hours, I walked Phoebe, changed her, and sat down to nurse her more times than my dazed head could count. The flight was still only half over. Flight attendants had dimmed the lights, and people across the plane wore peaceful sleeping faces. My watch set to U.S. time said midnight. This was the longest Phoebe had gone without sleep in her life. That was not the record either of us wanted to be setting.

"Excuse me," a flight attendant nudged me as I paced up and down the aisle. "Safety regulations say you *must* sit down." Phoebe's eyes had just begun to drop closed, and the

the mommy diaries

minute I sat in my seat, she jumped and wailed again. The man at my elbow lifted his eye mask and glared. I turned to the flight attendant and glared. I stood up and walked to the bathroom, pretending I would change Phoebe's diaper. I rocked her harder and harder. Still she wailed.

A woman stood next to me. I was too tired to speak, but I'm sure the look on my face told the story clearly enough. It was at that moment that this woman chose to say, "You have a beautiful baby." I was flabbergasted. Some words came out of my mouth, but I'm not sure if they made sense. Beautiful? She must not be on *this* plane, with *this* baby! Yet there she was, offering to hold the baby, talking to her and making those bloodshot baby eyes twinkle into a smile. And sure enough, I could remember now, Phoebe was a beautiful baby.

> And hope does not disappoint us, because God has poured out his love into our hearts by the Holy Spirit, whom he has given us.
>
> Romans 5:5

Upon arriving in China, I called my husband from a cell phone borrowed from a Chinese stranger. I choked out only a few words as all my emotions let loose into sobs— "I missed my flight. It's terrible. I'll call you later." With tears running down my face, I handed the phone back to the baffled stranger. I caught a taxi across Beijing to find a place to sleep, and finally I tucked a perfectly peaceful Phoebe into bed. The memories of that twenty-seven-hour day rushed out in a flood.

But the image of that woman stood firm in the midst of them all. Somehow she saw something beautiful in Phoebe, even at a baby's ugliest moment. And if she could see it in my baby, I realized God could see it even in me, even in my worst hours. When my bright-eyed child becomes a raging tiger and I feel like a tiger myself, still there is a God who always finds us beautiful. That God picks us up in the middle of our tantrums, rocks us, calms us, and sees us through.

Lost and Found
by Mária Carraseo Seifert

The day began with me stepping on my proverbial shoelace; it was quickly becoming "one of those days." I sat at my dining table trying to figure out how I got here, in this messy kitchen with two children . . . and the one thinks her mouth is on top of her head, because that is where she is feeding herself. I had recently stopped my career to become a stay-at-home mom. Need I say more? Being with my children day in and day out was more difficult than helping constituents navigate the sea of red tape within the federal government!

I remember daydreaming at my desk of having the opportunity to spend more time with my girls. Now here I was with my girls, in a "new to me" house in the suburbs. I'd worked my whole life and had no idea what I was doing raising these children we had on purpose. I didn't receive any training, nor did I attend any seminars or classes.

I made a mental note to go to Barnes & Noble to buy a parenting book and then thought of all the work it would take to get out of the house before the store closed. Not to mention the time it would take to read it when I couldn't even complete a thought these days. I threw my mental note in my mental wastebasket, which was beginning to overflow.

As if leaving a very successful career and moving to the suburbs miles away from my family wasn't bad enough, the

the mommy diaries

worst part was that I had no friends in the suburbs to help me through this rough patch. For the kajillionth time that morning I thought, "Poor me." I'd only been awake an hour.

Later that evening, a neighboring family came to our door to welcome us to the neighborhood. My house was sparkling clean, my husband and children were well dressed, and my kitchen smelled of roasted chicken when I greeted this family at the door. Right. In real life, we were eating Chinese take-out because I couldn't manage to get a grip on my day to have supper ready on time; toys, children's clothing, and half-unpacked moving boxes were scattered everywhere.

My husband Paul was working on something in the basement and had just come out of the bathroom with freshly washed hands that he neglected to dry completely in a rush to answer the door. He was wearing his threadbare college T-shirt that had at least a dozen holes in it. My three-year-old was sprinting around buck naked, and my eighteen-month-old had disappeared with a freshly fermenting diaper. The smell quickly permeated the entire main level of our home. Wouldn't it be nice if toddlers who require privacy for number two would take their diaper-clad bottoms into the bathroom and shut the door rather then hide somewhere in the house?

Thankfully the doorbell rang *again* and brought my attention back to the family on the other side of the door. Paul and I clunked heads while looking through the little hole in the front door. He turned to me, flustered, and said, "I'll look for her one more time, and *you* let them in!" He ran off and I opened the door, smiling graciously at my new friends. I asked them to come in, but only because it was 28 degrees outside.

The two preschool boys immediately held their noses but didn't say a word. Paul came into the kitchen, shrugging his shoulders as if to say "no luck," then turned to our guests and introduced himself. The guys shook hands and talked as if they weren't surrounded by a toe-curling odor. I took a seat and spoke with my new friend Sheila. At this point I noticed that my husband had forgotten to close his pants zipper, and two seconds after that, a naked little girl that resembled a peach-colored blur streaked through our kitchen. Again, the two little boys spoke nothing, but their eyebrows said it all. I pretended not to notice the blur and continued talking with my new friend, hoping that she didn't notice and that she didn't have a sense of smell. Sheila shared with me that she was a stay-at-home mom and had recently moved into the neighborhood. We became fast friends, and I was so grateful.

A few weeks later, Sheila invited me to attend a MOPS meeting at a church near our home. I jumped at the chance to meet other mothers who have taken on this humongous task of staying home to raise children. I'd make friends *and* learn something! When we arrived at the church, I removed my coat only to notice a bunch of crumbs cemented to the shoulder of my black sweater. I picked at it as quickly as I could in an attempt to look "put together" like everyone else. Something made me stop and look up. As I looked around the table at all the women in our group, all but two had stains, crumbs, or a white film on the shoulders of their shirts; two looked like they hadn't slept in days; and one looked like she had skipped a shower that morning. A feeling of indescribable peace poured over me; I was in the right place. These ladies were just like me.

the mommy diaries

At MOPS I learned about that feeling of peace—where it comes from and who gives it to us. I learned to love and appreciate my children and to see them as gifts from God, even when they make me nuts. I learned about the power of prayer reflected in my life and how humbling it is to have others pray for me. I learned that gossiping about and judging people is wrong. I learned about true Christian fellowship that is strong, stable, loyal, and trustworthy. I learned character accountability. I laughed out loud, I cried with these ladies, and we laid impenetrable foundations of friendship. Best of all, MOPS led me to learn about the gifts God gave me to fulfill my purpose here on Earth.

About a year after joining MOPS, I had a home party for a girlfriend and invited my old work friends as well as my new friends. I'll never forget my co-worker telling me, "Wow, I guess I'm really surprised you have so many friends and you are a stay-at-home mom!" That made me smile and respond, "I *am* blessed, aren't I?"

My Best Years
by Kathy Groom

I sat helplessly on the floor of our tiny living room, my three young children upset and crying. All three of them—all at the same time. My three-year-old screamed through tears for my attention—"MAMA!"—while her two-year-old brother and infant sister howled and sobbed at my feet. The hot Arizona sun streamed in the window, adding stifling heat to a frenzied situation.

Wanting to share this moment with my husband—the father of these little cherubs—I dialed my husband's work number and pointed the receiver in the general direction of our squalling children. Without uttering a word, I simply held the phone in the middle of the room, allowed his voicemail to record the broadcasted wailing for about ten seconds, and then hung up. Needless to say, he didn't return my call.

Completely unable to get myself together, I turned to the one place I was sure to get help. I called my mom. My dad answered instead. When he heard the chaos of his grandchildren in the background and the hysteria of his daughter, he laughed. Unsure whether his chuckle was steeped in fatherly understanding or sheer amusement, I heard myself wail through unstoppable panic, "I want my mama!"

Unfortunately, my mother was off shopping, no doubt thinking that her days of listening to her children whine were long over, so my dad began to ask me questions. I assured him my crisis included no blood or crime; I was just overwhelmed and I needed help. Dad listened and soon recognized the problem that I had failed to see.

"Honey, you need to let some things go," he said. "Enjoy your kids while you have them at home. These are the best years of your life." *Yeah, right, Dad. Easy for an empty-nester to say.*

The thought baffled me. I was working so hard to manage all the important things in my life; I couldn't imagine letting any of them go. *Except maybe the kids, my husband, and the dog,* I silently mused. Something had to change. "Thanks, Dad," I mumbled as I hung up. "I'll think about it."

After receiving my customized voicemail SOS, my brave husband came home to find me crumpled on the couch and the kids running amok. He bent down to check my pulse.

"Honey?" he nudged cautiously.

"I just can't take it anymore!" I yelled. "Why did we have so many kids?"

The wise man had no quick answer. Instead he gently said, "I'll take the kids to the neighbors'. Don't move."

When he returned, we knelt in front of our well-worn sofa and asked God for help. My husband grabbed a notebook and started writing down all the "stuff" I was trying to do. As we examined my responsibilities, we soon realized my dad was right. I was so busy with demands outside our home that chaos had overtaken inside. Reluctantly, I had to admit to myself that I wasn't enjoying these "best years" very much, and neither were my children.

With my dad's advice to "enjoy!" ringing in my ears, my husband and I started a list of what we thought was most important to us, moving intentional time with the kids toward the top of the list. Although many of the activities I had pursued were valuable and I enjoyed them, I realized they did not top our priorities. Not only that, but the weight of time and energy they consumed made me a completely ineffective and unhappy mom.

We decided I would resign immediately—from *everything*. I called the choir director, the chairman of the board, the children's ministry coordinator, everyone, and said, "I quit!" It was a drastic move, but it's one I have never regretted.

As my focus shifted back to my family, I went from super-stressed maniac to fun-and-available mom. On sunny days, instead of attending meetings, I hung out at the park with my kids for hours. On rainy days, we baked cookies or cuddled under layers of blankets, reading favorite storybooks. We blew monster bubbles at the children's museum and peered into revolving eyes at the tropical exhibit, and I treasured being with my children, all of us giddy with interest. When the children napped, I napped. With more rest, I found myself able to handle the demands of motherhood much better.

Through the years, I have continued to be intentional about enjoying my kids at every stage of their lives. We graduated from Candy Land to Monopoly to Nintendo Wii, but we still play. Story time evolved from pointing at Richard Scarry picture books to reading aloud together from C. S. Lewis's *Chronicles of Narnia* to watching *Lord of the Rings* movies. Sometimes I've had to try extra hard, but I have managed to find enjoyment in every stage of our children's development. And the results are worth it.

Our children are now teens and young adults, and just the other day our family shared a leisurely summer dinner on the front porch. We visited and laughed and simply enjoyed being together. As I listened to the kids reminisce and giggle about shared childhood experiences, my heart burst with pleasure. I had learned to focus and be intentional about what was most important in my life, and here we all were: talking, laughing, and loving. All of us—all at the same time.

The Little Boy Who Waves

by Michelle M. Guppy

On the first day of school, the yellow bus with the squeaky brakes stopped in front of our house. The attendant took my child's hand as he made his way up the steps into the bus. She told him, "Good morning! This is your seat." I stepped away from the door and went to the window where he was sitting. I tapped on the window, trying to get my son to look at me. He wouldn't. The fan on the dashboard had caught his attention, and there was no distracting him from that. I waved good-bye to him anyway.

As time went on, we had our routine down—both Brandon and I. I would guide him up the stairs of the bus, then go to the window to try to get him to look at me. He never would. I simply could not compete with the fan on the dashboard that fascinated him so. But I kept waving.

One day I noticed the other children sitting behind Brandon. One child would stare out the window as he was rocking back and forth. I wondered what he was thinking. He had such a serious, far-off expression on his face. One morning I noticed another child a couple rows behind him. As I waved to my son as the bus left, this particular child waved back. He was looking at me, waving and smiling.

And so began our new routine. Each morning after I would tap on the window and wave to my son, I would then turn and wave to this little boy. He actually appeared to be anticipating his turn to be "waved at."

That was our thing: every morning as the bus left, I would turn and wave to this little boy. I admit I am very jealous of this boy's mom. Every morning she gets a wave and smile from her son—and my son doesn't even know I am there waving at him. Once my son gets on the bus, his focus turns to the fan on the dashboard. Yet this little boy I now wave at too gives me hope that someday my child might notice me and wave to me with a smile. It is a very bittersweet moment each morning, but it is a hopeful moment as well. Many mornings I have walked back into my house in tears, pleading with God to make my child more like that child.

One morning I woke up on the wrong side of the bed. After I grumpily handed my child off to the attendant, I turned to go back inside. I didn't tap on the window to wave good-bye to my child—or anyone else's. As I got to my front door and was about to open it, something made me turn and look at the bus. There it was—a panic-stricken face pressed against the school bus window with a little hand waving frantically at me. A wave of guilt spread over me. I hastily stepped back and turned to wave back, but it was too late; I don't think the little boy who waves saw me.

Never again have I forgotten to wave to him. And I truly miss that little boy when he's not there to wave at me.

I was sick one morning, and my husband had to do the bus routine for me. As I was giving him instructions as to what to put in our son's backpack and so on, I told him about the little boy who waves in the sixth row—and made my husband promise me he wouldn't forget to wave at him.

"Why do you want me to wave at someone else's kid?" he asked me.

I didn't have the energy to explain my feelings to him right then. That the little boy was my hope, my inspiration, my prayer for my own son. That I do it because for that one moment, I imagine my son being the little boy who smiles and waves good-bye to me each morning. Instead I replied, "Just please . . ."

He said he would.

I would never trade my son for anyone else's. I thank God every day for my child and what he *can* do. But inside of me, I do long for the day when the "little boy who waves" could be mine.

Another school year came and went. The little boy in the sixth row was no longer on the bus, but still I waved at my son with the hope that he would wave to me. One day out of the blue, the attendant said to me, "You know, it's the cutest thing—whenever the bus starts moving, while your son is humming and watching the fan, he will hold his hand beside his leg and start opening and closing his fist like he is waving."

As it turned out, what I wished most desperately for had been there all along. And if I had given up looking for it, I never would have found it. I learned a powerful lesson about hope that day: it does not disappoint. Never give up hope. Have faith, because what may seem impossible just may be possible.

Hope Springs Eternal
by Paula Brunswick

I didn't become a mother until my mid-thirties, so I had plenty of time to dream about what motherhood would look like. One of the things I looked forward to was sitting on the floor, playing with my baby. By the time my first child was born, I had a small collection of brightly colored toys and board books. One of my friends gave me one of those quilts with sensory-stimulating toys attached, as well as an "A-frame" with dangling toys. I couldn't wait for playtime!

the mommy diaries

But then my dreams crashed into reality. When Sarah was three days old, I seriously injured my lower back. The doctor thought I would get better within a few weeks, but the weeks ultimately stretched into months. I was in excruciating pain most of the time, and looking back I realize I was also suffering from depression, so I didn't have the emotional or mental ability to seek the medical care I needed. We had one wing chair where I could sit comfortably with a support pillow, but sitting on the floor was out of the question.

When Sarah got old enough to be interested in the toys, I would lay her down on the quilt and talk to her from the wing chair. But every time I tried this, I was overcome with the pain of disappointment. Sometimes I would cry. Sometimes I would feel angry that such a simple dream was lost to me. Sometimes I would feel guilty because I felt like a bad mom. Always I would pray and ask God to take away the pain.

The pain continued, and Sarah soon grew big enough that I couldn't manage picking her up from the floor. We had moved to a new city just before Sarah was born, so I didn't have any friends or family to call on, and my husband was at work all day. I had signed up for MOPS but didn't go because I couldn't comfortably sit anywhere but the old green wing chair. If only I had known then what I know now about MOPS, I would have called in a heartbeat and had all the friends and help I needed! What I did know was that Sarah needed that time on the floor, kicking and exploring, and she needed her mom to interact with her. I needed it too. How was I going to manage?

One day as I sat nursing Sarah, I prayed and asked God not to take the pain away but to grant me the courage and wisdom to cope well with my situation, to be the mom I needed to be in spite of my inadequacies. It occurred to me that I could lie down on my side or my back next to Sarah. That way I could hold up a book and read it, help her play with the dangling toys, or hand her a new rattle. I could get down on the floor in stages—kneeling on the floor, moving her from the couch to the quilt, pulling the quilt over to an open space, lying down beside her, and reversing the process when it was time to get up. It worked!

It was a turning point for me. Instead of tears, anger, and guilt, I found hope. I realized that if I could figure out how to overcome this hurdle, then I could figure out how to overcome other ways my back pain was limiting me. I decided to try MOPS and discovered that instead of the metal folding chairs I had envisioned, they had cushioned chairs with a full back that would accommodate my lumbar pillow. I started making new friends. I made an appointment with a specialist and finally got the right diagnosis for my back pain along with the appropriate treatment. And most importantly of all, I got to realize my dream! I still have vivid memories of Sarah kicking her legs and chuckling with delight as I joined her on the floor.

> The pessimist sees difficulty in every opportunity. The optimist sees the opportunity in every difficulty.
> —Winston Churchill

At thirty-three, I had had plenty of opportunities to learn that the reality of life sometimes disappoints our dreams, but as a mom I came to understand in a deeper way the importance of bringing hope out of disappointment—for my own sake and that of my family. I learned that a little creativity and perseverance can not just change the disappointment at hand but also give us the courage to recognize and tackle other challenges.

Hope in the Eyes of a Child
by Luisel Lawler

Charlie was a special boy with special needs. The moment I met him he stole my heart. He was autistic, but that never stopped him from experiencing life to the fullest. His joy was evident to all who knew him. His big smile and piercing blue-green eyes were unforgettable. He won the hearts of all who came around him.

And then tragedy struck on his sixth birthday. An accidental dose of the wrong prescription took his life. As the reality sunk in that he was gone, heaviness filled my heart, as did many unanswered questions. I knew I had to explain it to my son Josh and the forty other children who were in class with Charlie at church. They loved him, and their hearts connected with Charlie even though they could not communicate with him.

When I gathered them together that Sunday morning, I could tell that many of them had already heard but some were not aware. Once they knew, sadness filled the room. We talked about our bodies being a shell that houses who we are—our soul. We talked about eternal life—how we will never die, even if our earthly body does, and that one day we will receive a heavenly body that is perfect in every way. We talked about what heaven is like, and the children started to share what it must be like for Charlie now. They said, "He's not sick anymore!" "He will never be sad and

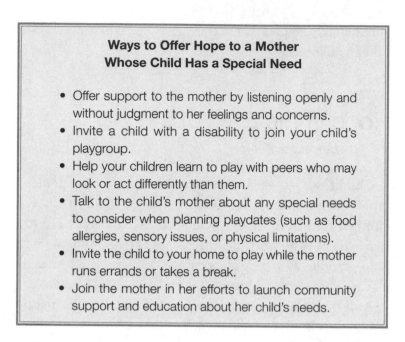

**Ways to Offer Hope to a Mother
Whose Child Has a Special Need**

- Offer support to the mother by listening openly and without judgment to her feelings and concerns.
- Invite a child with a disability to join your child's playgroup.
- Help your children learn to play with peers who may look or act differently than them.
- Talk to the child's mother about any special needs to consider when planning playdates (such as food allergies, sensory issues, or physical limitations).
- Invite the child to your home to play while the mother runs errands or takes a break.
- Join the mother in her efforts to launch community support and education about her child's needs.

cry anymore!" "And he does not need any more medicine." "He is with God and the angels singing praises." I watched my son, Josh, as understanding dawned on his face and he exclaimed, "Charlie can talk now!" Another child said, "It is beautiful in heaven, with the streets of gold and jewels. It is better than any place we have ever been, even Chuck E. Cheese's. Charlie must love it there."

As their faces lifted from the sadness to the reality of heaven, we talked about each of them going there one day if they have asked Jesus to be their Savior. We talked about how they would see Charlie again and never, ever have to say good-bye again. They talked about how Charlie would tell them what he had been doing while he was there.

What started as something sad ended as something hopeful because of the promises we have through Jesus Christ.

the mommy diaries

As I looked at their faces, I realized that these children understood better than I did. They understood where our hope lies. Charlie is where we all hope and long to be: in the presence of God, whole and happier than we can imagine. These children helped me see that the troubles of this world are temporary. What really matters is eternity. They helped me to adjust my focus on the hope we have. Yes, I can grieve for the loss of time with Charlie, but I still smile when I think of where he is and that I will see him again. Why would I want anything else for him than what he has now? Charlie is finally home.

Refuge in a Storm
by Rhonda Headley

My girls and I tumbled into the car in happy anticipation of an afternoon birthday party. We were going to pick up Grandma and then proceed to my cousin's house for the celebration. It was a hot August afternoon, and the skies began to threaten as we were en route on the expressway. Suddenly we heard a clap of thunder, and a summer pop-up thunderstorm was upon us. The rain-heavy clouds dumped their load on us in grand fashion, so I quickly switched on the headlights and the windshield wipers.

The wipers were working furiously in the downpour as we continued, somewhat more slowly, on our way. Then something went terribly wrong. The windshield wipers suddenly and inexplicably stopped and were frozen mid-windshield. I scrambled to jiggle the wiper switch, to no avail, as my mind raced in a panic to survey my options. We were still moving in traffic, and there wasn't a proper shoulder onto which to pull over safely. We traveled this stretch of highway frequently, so I knew we were approaching an exit, but visibility in the downpour was incredibly poor. I was scared we were going to wreck or cause an accident, and the fear became palpable in the backseat once the girls were aware of our situation as well.

Frantically, I put on the emergency flashers and rolled down the window. With rain streaming in my face, I somehow managed to look out both the open driver's side window and whatever spot I could see through on the windshield as I maneuvered us slowly off the exit and into the first parking lot I approached. All the while, the girls prayed audibly for our safety as I tried rather unsuccessfully to exude calm.

> God tells us to burden him with whatever burdens us.
>
> —Unknown

As if on cue, moments after parking, the rain stopped and the storm blew past. We were blessedly safe, but I was too shaken to continue to the party. I couldn't risk another pop-up storm, and I was still baffled by the malfunction of the wipers. I later learned that the wiper motor had blown and needed to be replaced, something mechanics rarely encounter.

How many times before had I turned on windshield wipers while driving in rain? Never once did I ever imagine they would fail me, especially in a storm. I never gave them a second thought. They're just supposed to work, like a chair is supposed to hold you when you sit down upon it. It's one of those things you don't think about. Wet and utterly relieved, I learned in a heart-pounding moment just who and what I could depend on. I learned that only my God is dependable and trustworthy without question, and I'm reminded of this lesson each time a drop hits the windshield.

Believing Prayers
by Kathi Macias

On a rare golden autumn day in the Pacific Northwest, my then two-year-old son, Chris, taught me the meaning of faith. I had taken him to the park for a picnic. As I unloaded the car, he ran ahead, looking for the playground. Suddenly I sensed that something was very wrong.

I dropped everything and began to run, praying for God's divine protection. Then I saw the slide. Chris had almost reached the top, climbing quickly and squealing with delight. Just as he got to the last rung he slipped, falling backward, headfirst, to the pavement below. Then, in that split second before he hit the ground, it was as if a cushion of feathers had been placed beneath him. He landed softly, bouncing up and looking at me quizzically, as if wondering why I was so upset.

I grabbed him and cried, "Chris, are you all right?"

He answered very simply, "Mom, the angels catched me." And off he went to play.

As I stood there staring after my son, I wondered, *Why am I so amazed? Why do I pray if I don't really believe God will answer?*

And then I remembered an illustration I had once heard a pastor give about "believing prayers." A woman was having doubts about what God could (or would) do in answer to prayer, so she decided to put him to the test. She got down on her knees one night and began to pray, "God, if you can hear me, remove that tree outside my window."

On and on she prayed until, as the morning light came softly through the window, she arose and looked outside. "Aha!" she exclaimed. "Just as I thought! It's still there."

> Prayer is exhaling the spirit of man and inhaling the spirit of God.
>
> —Edwin Keith

I realized how much I had been like that woman when I prayed—mouthing the words but not really expecting an answer. Oh, I know God's answer won't always be yes, but he does hear, he does care, and—as I humbly learned from a two-year-old—he always answers believing prayers.

Unexpected Hope
by Elisabeth Selzer

"Mama! Mama!" Joey, my rambunctious eighteen-month-old, tugged mercilessly on the edge of my sweater. I looked down and noticed a dark bruise the size of a nickel on his chubby forearm. I didn't remember the tears which the tumble that caused it certainly would have brought. I dismissed this thought as I noticed the diaper explosion evidenced on his yellow T-shirt that more urgently needed my attention. I carried him at arm's length to the changing table and quickly took off the little boots which had carried him around the gravel playground just an hour earlier. As I peeled his dirt-streaked socks off, my heart jumped into my throat. His feet were covered in violet and crimson bruises.

the mommy diaries

I rewound my tape to that morning, when I had written off the bloody spot on his teddy bear sheets. I thought he had hit his mouth on the crib—the evidence of dried blood had been on his lip that morning. But now I wondered if this was all somehow connected. The blood spot had been bigger than a little bump would have warranted. Panic began to take over as I remembered the anxiety that simple bruises gave my mother when I was a little girl, brought on by the pain and grief she had suffered when my seven-year-old brother had died of leukemia.

I heard my husband, Steve, walk in the front door, home uncharacteristically early from work. I yelled for him to come into Joey's room, the pitch of my voice giving away my fear. Within minutes of Steve seeing Joey's feet and the other bruises I had noticed while changing Joey, we were racing to the emergency room.

The ER attendant took one look at Joey and immediately rushed us back to a room where they threw questions at us like stones. Once they were satisfied his condition was not due to abuse, the medical tests began in earnest. The waiting was a gauntlet that seemed unbearable. All I could think about was that I needed to talk to my mom. The waiting room phone was free, but my hands were shaking so much that I feared I wouldn't dial the right number. She answered after one ring, and the sound of her voice brought on the flood of tears I had kept at bay until now. Through sobs I told her about my precious son, so helpless and so sick.

She listened until I was spent. Then she began to comfort me with the caring words of a mother. She finished the conversation by asking me if she could pray with me. I weakly agreed. Her prayerful words were like a blanket of reassurance and quiet peace. She then asked me if she could call our family members and her group of friends to pray for us as well. I hesitated at first, thinking this wasn't their problem to be concerned with, but in desperation I agreed.

We sat and waited for a diagnosis, watching Joey in his Elmo hospital gown play with the stuffed Tasmanian devil he had been given for his bravery in enduring a spinal tap. Oddly, the faces of my family and the faces I imagined of these praying friends my mom had mentioned earlier entered my consciousness, easing to a degree the fear that seemed to have taken on a life of its own. I felt an indescribable peace holding me with the thought that so many were caring about a young, frightened family in a remote ER.

Finally we received the diagnosis: Idiopathic thrombocytopenic purpura (ITP), a condition in which the body quits making the platelets which allow blood to clot. Any bump or cut would cause immediate bleeding without the ability to stop. Just the pressure of Joey's shoes on his feet had caused the capillaries to break and the bruises to cover them in a red and purple blur. In a chilling statement, the doctor said that if Joey had fallen off the play equipment he had joyously climbed on earlier that day, he very well could have died. As I listened to this frightening diagnosis, I felt the comfort and care of those praying for us again. And something much more profound surrounded their care: the presence of God infusing this moment suspended in time.

Joey would face a few difficult months of strong medicines, checkups, and us keeping him in a bicycle helmet and off anything twelve inches or higher—no small feat with a busy toddler. As these months slowly passed, the care of our family and friends continued, sometimes through cards of encouragement,

the mommy diaries

sometimes through messages sent through my mom. I felt unworthy, and yet they helped us to keep going.

Joey is now fourteen and has not had a recurrence of ITP since he was that rough-and-tumble toddler. But the lesson of hope which a dedicated group of people gave me still encourages me to believe in something bigger than myself—a caring God who touches us through people and their prayers for us. A loving God who uses the kindness and concern of people to be our support when we face a world that feels like it is caving in.

Discovering Hope . . . Every Day

When we face challenges or even the most tragic circumstances, we often aren't even aware of hope's presence in the midst of our struggle. But subtly and ever so gently, we find ourselves moving away from the dark of doubt and into the warm glow of hope. Somehow life changes and we find meaning where we once found nihilism, purpose where we once found waste, abundance where we once found destitution.

No matter where we find ourselves along the mothering journey, we can surely trust that our rescuer will come, our companion hasn't deserted us. He is there during the joyful patches, when our road is dappled with sunlight. He is there during the desperate times, when night falls thick and heavy. And through it all, we can push on with confidence because we know for certain that hope *does not* disappoint.

Expanding Your Limit

1. What are some of the hardest times during your mothering journey to trust that hope exists?
2. When life gets dark, is it hard for you to lean on hope for help? Why?
3. When have you seen hope in action, bringing you from a place of doubt to a place of promise?
4. Where do you find your sources for hope? Do they shift and change, or do they remain eternally steadfast?
5. Are there parts of your life that are keeping you from embracing hope? What would it take to overcome those issues and bring you into a place of hope?

the mommy diaries

Acknowledgments

Writing and compiling a book involves many people, just like the daily adventure of mothering is not a solitary pursuit.

Tally Flint was supported in her writing by her darlings, Thomas, Ella, and the twin babes, and most of all by Ryan, her best friend and lifetime love.

Julie Cantrell provided an amazing array of sidebars and information gleaned from her own adventurous family, tireless research, and connections with many moms.

Mary Beth Lagerborg launched the idea for this book and is now continuing in her own adventure, while Jean Blackmer, with the assistance of Jackie Alvarez, brought the final product to print for MOPS International. The leadership of Elisa Morgan, Naomi Cramer Overton, and Carla Foote make the publishing work at MOPS International possible.

Lee Hough of Alive Communications and the wonderful people at Revell, including Jennifer Leep, Twila Bennett, and Suzie Cross, each had a hand in the adventure of putting the book together. They are great partners in publishing.

Of course, the moms who contributed stories to the book represent the daily adventure of mothering. We thank each mom for being vulnerable in her story. It is our hope that through these stories, you will gain perspective on what you are learning about yourself as a woman and mother in the midst of your adventure.

Contributors

Crystal Bowman is a bestselling author of over fifty books for children including *The One Year Book of Devotions for Preschoolers*, *The House in the Middle of Town*, and *J is for Jesus*. She speaks at local MOPS groups and is a mentoring mom at her church in Florida.

Laura Broadwater—motherhood—that's a job that's changed my life forever.

Paula Brunswick enjoys the daily adventure with her husband, Bob, and their children, Sarah and Ryan, in Flagstaff, Arizona. After being deeply impacted by the MOPS ministry as a new mom, Paula has welcomed the chance to give back by serving as a field leader for over seven years.

Elsa Kok Colopy is the author of four books and hundreds of articles. She also speaks regularly at retreats and conferences. For more information, visit www.elsakokcolopy.com.

Scoti Springfield Domeij was propelled into solo parenthood with two sons ages four and nine months. She authored *Favorite Bible Heroes* and coauthored *Wrong Way, Jonah* with Kay Arthur. She's been published in the *New York Times*, *Focus on the Family* magazine, *Contemporary Christian Music*, *Southwest Art*, and other parenting magazines.

Karen Ehman is a wife, mother of three, national speaker for Proverbs 31 Ministries, and author of four books, including *The Complete Guide to Getting and Staying Organized*. She has been a guest on national television and radio programs including *The 700 Club* and *Focus on the Family*.

Tally Flint has nearly ten years experience as a writer and editor. She and her husband live with their four children, ages four and under, in Denver, Colorado.

Carla Foote is the director of media for MOPS International and has responsibility for the magazine, book, and Web publishing functions. She is the editor of *FullFill* magazine (www.FullFill.org). Carla and her husband Dave have two children and a half-empty nest.

Kari J. Glemaker is the national director for *iCare*, a women's prayer movement to educate parents and family members of the dangers of our sexualized society through ever-changing technology. Kari and her husband Dave live with their three children in a suburb of Cincinnati. Kari is an avid sports fan, loves to scrapbook, and reads anything she can get her hands on.

Angie Grella is a stay-at-home mom and a part-time piano teacher. She is married to Chris, and they have two sons, Nathan (7) and Joshua (5). She would like to dedicate her story to her mother, Sharon Bruckner, who died of cancer in 2003.

Elizabeth Griffin lives with her husband and sons near Seattle. She works as a reporter for *Journal Newspapers* (www.journal-newspapers.com) and has written two books, *Fragile X, Fragile Hope* about her disabled son and *Margot's Story* about one family's survival during World War II. Elizabeth enjoys teaching and public speaking.

In her early years of parenting, **Kathy Groom** chose to apply her community service degree as a stay-at-home mom. Now that her four children are nearly grown, Kathy is founder and president of Prayer Sisters International, a ministry designed to help women connect in friendship and prayer support (www.prayersisters.org).

Rebecca K. Grosenbach lives in Colorado Springs with her husband and three children. A former editor for *Today's Christian Woman* magazine, Rebecca works part-time as a writer for the Navigators, a

Christian discipleship ministry. She also speaks at women's retreats, MOPS groups, and other events.

Sara Groves, a singer/songwriter and MOP, lives in Minneapolis with her husband Troy and kids Kirby, Toby, and Ruby.

Michelle M. Guppy of Houston, Texas, is married to Todd and has two kids, Matthew (15) and Brandon (14). She is an advocate of Texas Autism Advocacy (www.TexasAutismAdvocacy.org) and can be reached at MichelleMGuppy@yahoo.com.

English major **Rhonda Headley** delights in making a home with her librarian husband of eleven years in Cincinnati. They have two daughters, ages five and eight, who love to read and write as much as their parents do. Rhonda currently serves as a council coordinator for MOPS International.

Liz Curtis Higgs is the bestselling author of *Bad Girls of the Bible, The Pumpkin Patch Parable, Thorn in My Heart,* and twenty-four other titles. She has presented fifteen hundred inspirational programs for audiences worldwide. She lives with her husband and two grown children in Kentucky. Visit her website www.LizCurtisHiggs.com.

Susan Hitts is a MOPS council coordinator in northern Michigan. Through MOPS, she has enjoyed speaking and writing about many preschool mothering topics. Susan and her husband, Randy, parent Angela, Teresa, Sarah, Elisa, and David. They also have a new baby due this July. Susan may be contacted at missburtlake@aol.com.

Diane Jasper is a retired teacher who is the recipient of two Ink of the Scribe awards. She is published in *MomSense* magazine and *Coal to Diamonds: True Stories of Triumph.* She writes children's books and inspirational stories from her ranch in the mountains near Cle Elum, Washington.

Christine Jeske, her husband Adam and their two children Phoebe and Ezekiel (Zeke) now live in South Africa, where they direct a micro-finance project. Christine discovered MOPS through a book given by a friend in China. She has written for several magazines and hopes to publish a book on motherhood. See more at www.jeskelife.org.

Contributors

Colleen Kappeler is a writer and stay-at-home mom for Henry (7) and Lucy (3). She writes, teaches, and edits in her "free" time. Visit Colleen's website www.colleenkappeler.com.

Jami Kirkbride enjoys her mothering adventures on a Wyoming ranch where she's inspired by her husband Jeff and four wonderful children. She uses her master's degree in counseling in her freelance writing, speaking, and personality training. Jami is also a contributing author to *Laundry Tales* and *When God Steps In*. Visit Jami at JamiKirkbride.com.

Alexandra (Alex) Kuykendall is mother to two preschoolers and has been known to shed tears at her local MOPS group in Denver, Colorado. She spends part of her week at the MOPS International office supporting MOPS groups and their leaders.

Carol Kuykendall is consulting editor for MOPS International's *MomSense* magazine. She is the author of four books, including *Five Simple Ways to Grow a Great Family*, and coauthor of five more, including *What Every Mom Needs*. Carol also writes for *Daily Guideposts* and is a popular speaker. She and her husband Lynn live in Boulder, Colorado.

Mary Beth Lagerborg is a writer and speaker who served as publishing manager for MOPS International and helped to craft more than seventy books. She is coauthor of the bestselling *Once-a-Month Cooking*, and her latest book is *Dwelling: Living Fully from the Space You Call Home*. Visit her blog at dwellingspace.com.

Luisel Lawler is a mother of five and serves with her husband Dave at Grace Fellowship. Her ministries include preschool director, Praying with Expectancy (expectant moms), and mentoring women through life's journey (www.luisellawler.com). Family, faith, and following God's plan are her passions. Her story is dedicated to the Van Alstines in memory of Charlie.

Kathi Macias is an award-winning author of more than twenty books. She is also a popular conference and retreat speaker. Her book *Moth-*

ers of the Bible Speak to Mothers Today releases in Spring 2009. She and her husband Al live in Homeland, California.

Karen Marchant is the director of development for MOPS International. She received her BA from David Lipscomb University in speech/communication and political science and previously served as the Tennessee House Republican press secretary. Karen and her husband Jeff have three awesome grown children and live in Highlands Ranch, Colorado.

Elisa Morgan (MDiv) is CEO of MOPS International, wife to Evan, mother to Eva and Ethan, and "Yia Yia" to Marcus.

Amy Nappa is a bestselling and award-winning author, cofounder of Nappaland.com, "the Free e-magazine for families," and a recovering chocoholic.

Michelle Ottoes is a Wyoming native who currently lives in Cheyenne, Wyoming, with her husband and daughters Alyson and Emily. They spent three years in San Antonio, Texas, where joining MOPS at Concordia Lutheran church was a lifesaver in a new city, giving her friends, support, and a stronger faith.

Naomi Cramer Overton is the president of MOPS International and is pursuing a seminary master's degree. She adores her husband of twenty-two years and their three children: Tyler, Delaney, and Katriel. With her kids, she likes to read, cook, make messes, create music, and hike. One day she aspires to exhaust her dog, Coco Loco.

Celeste Palermo lives in Colorado with her husband Pete and daughters Peyton and Morgan. She is the author of *From the Red Tees: Help, Hope, and Humor for Women on the Green* and a devotional book for moms coming out in 2009. She writes for various magazines and her local newspaper. Visit her at www.celestepalermo.com.

Leslie Parrott (EdD) is cofounder (with her husband Les) of the Center for Relationship Development at Seattle Pacific University and the author of *Your Time-Starved Marriage, Love Talk, God Made You Nose to Toes* (children's book), and *You Matter More Than You Think*. Visit Leslie's speaking schedule at www.RealRelationships.com.

Contributors

Cathy Penshorn is the author of *Juggling Tasks, Tots, and Time*, released by MOPS International in 2001. She lives with her husband and three sons near San Antonio, Texas, and speaks often to MOPS groups and women's groups around the state.

Over the past eight years MOPS has provided **Jennifer Prince** with many opportunities to serve preschool mothers. She and her husband Earl reside in Forest, Virginia, where Jennifer pursues her interests in world missions, entertaining, and journaling about her experiences in parenting her children Aubrey, William, and Hadley.

Shelly Radic is director of ministry life at MOPS International. She lives in Colorado with her husband and four children.

Jane Rubietta is a mother of three. She and her husband Rich lead Abounding Ministries. Jane is a speaker and author of ten books, most recently *Come Closer: A Call to Life, Love and Breakfast on the Beach*. For more information see www.JaneRubietta.com.

Mária Carraseo Seifert is a writer who provides humorous, soul-seeking messages through her writing. Mária lives with her husband Paul and their three children in New Berlin, Wisconsin. They attend Elmbrook Church.

Dr. Elisabeth (Liz) Selzer is the director of leadership development for MOPS International and the executive editor of *FullFill* magazine. She has a passion for equipping women to recognize, utilize, and maximize the influence they have. Liz has worked in ministry for over twenty-three years and is an adjunct professor at several universities.

Cheryl L. Steplight is currently homeschooling her three children. She is also pursuing a MDiv from Bethel Theological Seminary in St. Paul, Minnesota. Although her passion is teaching God's Word, her first ministry is to her husband and family. Cheryl and her family reside in Washington, DC.

Ronica Stromberg is the author of a picture book, *The Time-for-Bed Angel*, and *The Glass Inheritance*, a mystery for 10- to 14-year-olds. Google Ronica's name to read more about her writing.

Letitia Suk speaks and writes for women on the topics of personal renewal and family life. She is also a personal life coach and inspires women to live the abundant life (www.moreoflifecoaching.com). She and her husband Tom live in Evanston, Illinois, and are the parents of four adult children.

Laryssa Toomer is a Bible teacher, writer, and speaker for women's conferences and MOPS groups. She is a contributing author to *A Cup of Comfort Devotional for Mothers.* A proud Army wife to Jeff and mother to three, Laryssa enjoys cooking and race walking. She resides in Fayetteville, North Carolina. Visit her at www.laryssatoomer.com.

Barbara Vogelgesang and her husband Jim are the proud parents of Nick, Libby, Sarah, and Alex. She is passionate about drawing families closer to each other and Jesus through her speaking, writing, and performing. Her motto is, "life is an exciting adventure." You can reach Barbara at imaginatory@entermail.net.

Beth K. Vogt is the author of *Baby Changes Everything: Embracing and Preparing for Motherhood after 35.* She is the editor of Connections, MOPS' leadership magazine, and has written for *MomSense, Discipleship Journal,* and Crosswalk.com. Beth and her husband live in Colorado Springs. They have four children—and one "daughter-in-love."

A newspaper reporter for twelve years, **Susan Besze Wallace** now does her best to cover the adventures of Zach (6), Luke (3), A.J. (1½), and Todd, her best friend and husband of fourteen years. A contributor to *MomSense* magazine, Susan is the author of an upcoming early mothering book series for MOPS International.

Mom of Azalea (4) and Asher (2), **Ginny Mooney Withrow** writes to keep her sanity and remind herself and other moms that we are all, by God's grace, on this adventure of motherhood together. She lives in Atlanta, Georgia.

Jeanne Zornes became a mom in her late thirties, and her two children are now young adults. A speaker and prolific author, she lives in Wenatchee, Washington. Her books include *When I Prayed for Patience . . . God Let Me Have It!* Learn more at www.awsawomen .com/awsadirectory.

190   Contributors